July 31, 2006

To Martha:

My wonderful Sister-in-law,
and to everyone in my special
Washington Family. I love you all.

Ann

Chesapeake & Ohio
Steam in Color as Modeled

By Dan Zugelter

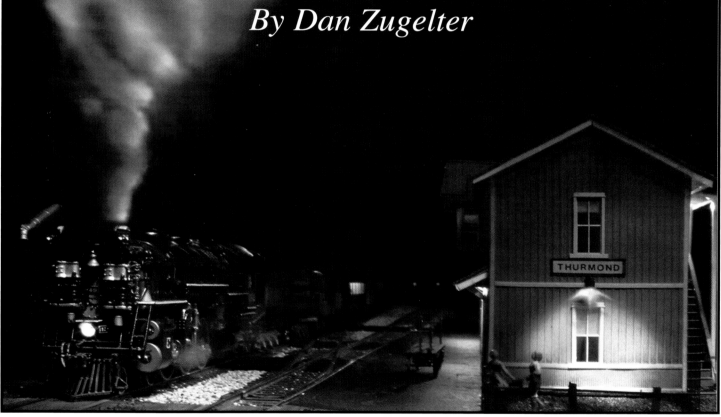

It's exactly 2:00 am. The westbound George Washington, headed by a spiffy Pacific (4-6-2) engine is right on time, and has just stopped at Thurmond. Only one passenger, an accountant for the Berwind Coal Company, is getting off. He will walk down the main street of Thurmond to the Hotel Lafayette (formerly the Thurmond Hotel) to register for some sleep before meeting tomorrow with Berwind's local manager. The engineer has not bothered to lower his headlight to dim, for in less than a minute he will be on his way.

Acknowledgments

I particularly wish to thank and acknowledge the endless help received from the following:

Mr. Nat Huggins, who built numerous structures to museum quality: the Thurmond Hotel, Armour meatpacking plant in Thurmond. In Sewell, the red row houses, general store, saloon, freight station and supervisor's house, in addition to planting a "million" trees.

Dr. James EuDaly has been my mentor for many years. He is a walking C&O encyclopedia; in addition, he has the finest "O" scale layout of the C&O that I will ever hope to see.

Ken Throckmorton also models the C&O in "N" scale. Ken can never do too much to help me, particularly in keeping these cantankerous steam engines running.

Dennis Realley has been a great help in beautiful automobile kits, passenger cars and trackwork.

Jack Fitzgerald is also a C&O modeler in "HO" scale. Jack's knowledge of electronics was invaluable in designing and assisting in the wiring of the signal systems.

Thomas W. Dixon, Jr. is the founder, President, Chairman and guiding light of the Chesapeake & Ohio Historical Society. Without Tom, the archives and the records that have been preserved without which the accuracy of the layout would have been impossible.

To my wife, Ann Zugelter, without whom I could not have produced this book on the model railroad.

International Standard Book Number: 0-939487-76-4

Design & Layout by
Megan Johnson
Johnson 2 Studios, Rustburg, Va.

Printed in USA
by Walsworth Publishing Co., Marceline, Mo.

Front Cover Captions: The FFV headed by beautiful Pacific (4-6-2) is seen crossing the New River approaching Sewell, W. Va.
Two giant H-7's (2-8-8-2) meet just west of C.W. Cabin, the western entrance to the Hinton yards. Eastbound train, to the left, is a loaded coal drag. Westbound train, to the right, has just left Hinton yards with empty hopper cars going back to the mines.

Contents

CHESAPEAKE AND OHIO RAILWAY
THE NEW RIVER AND ALLEGHANY SUBDIVISIONS

In time-honored manner C&O locomotives are serviced in
and around the coaling station at Hinton, W. Va.

Introduction

Please think of this book, not as about a model railroad, but as a historical revision of selected points of interest in 100 miles of the Chesapeake and Ohio Railway, New River and Alleghany Subdivisions as they were in the summer of 1938. We are not attempting to look beyond 1938. 1938 is the present time.

Unfortunately, the people, towns and particularly the steam engines of the time are mostly gone today. Fortunately, though historical records and plans have been preserved, so that these places can be recreated in miniature for our enjoyment.

WHY THE CHESAPEAKE AND OHIO?

Many years ago, I was attracted to the C&O by the unique look of their steam engines. The headlights were placed low on the front of the engine. Above the headlight were the air pumps - one on each side of the front of the smoke box. Normally these air pumps are on the side of the engine. However, in the 1920's, the C&O needed larger engines to accommodate heavier and longer trains. At that time the tunnels were not large enough for these bigger engines. By moving the air pumps from the side of the engines to the front, a little additional clearance in the tunnels was achieved. In turn, the bell was mounted above the air pumps. To complete the picture, many of the engines had an Elesco feed water heater mounted at the top of the engine smoke box. (This is for the purpose of preheating the water before it goes in the boiler for better efficiency.) Putting this all together produced a quite unique C&O look, that some called a Georgian architectural look. By coincidence many of the new passenger stations being built by the C&O at this time were a beautiful classic Georgian architecture. Well, whatever, a beautiful steam engine can only be in the eyes of the beholder.

Interestingly, by he late 1930's, when the tunnels were enlarged, or new larger tunnels built, the C&O shop crews so liked the look that they kept mounting the headlights down low even though it was no longer necessary.

WHY 1938?

The country was still in the grip of the great depression. Unlike most businesses and railroads, the C&O was very profitable. Coal was king and labor was cheap. Hauling coal has always been the most profitable and stable part of the railroad business, and the C&O was primarily a coal-hauling railroad. When the C&O was built during the 1870's and 1880's, coal-haul-

ing was not an interest. It was built to connect the Atlantic seaboard with the Ohio valley, and hopefully to be part of a transcontinental railroad. The latter never happened. In the process of building through West Virginia, mountains of good bituminous coal were discovered. This was just in time for America's booming industrial revolution; the rest became history.

During the depression years in West Virginia, by far, the best jobs were working for the railway. The employees were happy to have a job and took great pride in their railway and the equipment. The engines were literally spit-and-polished, as can be clearly seen in pictures of the day. This produced a very upbeat picture of prosperity. In fact, when one looks over pictures of steam engines, if the engines are clean and polished you can almost bet the pictures were taken in the 1930's. If not, the pictures were from the 1940's and 1950's. (During the war years, the C&O was too busy to do anything but just keep 'em running.)

In 1938, the C&O had many passenger trains. There were three daily name passenger trains between Cincinnati and Washington. Since the railway was on a solid financial basis they could lavish money on these "pride of the railway" trains. In addition, there were numerous mail and express trains and local passenger trains. There were many merchandise express freight trains and also local freight trains that stopped at almost every station with less-than-carload lots of freight (LCL). In addition to all of these scheduled passenger and freight trains , there was a steady stream of coal drags going east and empty hopper trains returning west.

The branches were not only active in bringing out coal, but many still had branch line passenger trains to serve the families in the "hollows."

This all resulted in a very busy railway, and the railroad was really a part of everyone's life.

WHY HINTON?

Hinton is near the western base of the Alleghany Mountains. In the steam era, all engines and crews were changed at Hinton. This was because larger engines had to be put on the trains, both passenger and freight, for the pull going east over the mountains. This is the Alleghany Subdivision. To the west the railway followed the New River, which was relatively level. Smaller, more efficient engines could be used here. This is the New River Subdivision.

Hinton was a very busy place; 75 to 100 engines every day, 24 hours per day, were changed and serviced here. Just look at the Employee Time Tables of 1938 for the New River and Alleghany Subdivisions, showing the number of First Class, Second Class and Third Class scheduled trains! In addition, there are about six coal trains in each direction each day that ran as unscheduled extras.

The First Class trains were:
The George Washington, Westward, No. 1; Eastward No. 2
The FFV   Westward No. 3; Eastward No. 6
The Sportsman   Westward No. 47; Eastward No. 4
Mail and Express   Westward No.15; Eastward No. 16
    The Second Class trains were local passenger trains.
    The Third Class trains were manifest fast freight trains.

I hope you will enjoy railfanning together on the C&O in the summer of 1938.

Dan Zugelter

Management has lined up in the Hinton yards from left to right three freight engines, an H7 (2-8-8-2), an H4 (2-6-6-2) a K-3 a (2-8-2) and two passenger engines, J-2 (4-8-2) and a F-17 (4-6-2.) They all illustrate the classic Georgian look of 1938. (Bernard Kempinski)

For a close-up individual look at these engines, we took the following pictures. Here is an H-7 (2-8-8-2) for heavy mainline freight service. (Bernard Kempinski)

This is an H-4 (2-6-6-2), the workhorse of the many branches to the coal mines. (Bernard Kempinski)

The K-3 Makado, with that great Georgian look, is the mainstay of the fast freights and local freights of the low gradient mainlines, such as the New River Subdivision. (Bernard Kempinski)

Mainline passenger trains, the FFV, Sportsman, and George Washington are under the charge of these beautiful F-19 Pacifics (4-6-2) on the New River Subdivision. (Bernard Kempinski)

On the steeper Mountain Subdivision, passenger power is turned over to a J-2 Mountain (4-8-2). (Bernard Kempinski)

In 1935, the first five J-3's (4-8-4) were received. In 1938, the headlight is still in the middle of the smoke box as received from the builder; it was later lowered to the bottom of the smoke box like its sisters. (Paul Dolkos)

The Main Street C&O Station in Charlottesville, VA is a good example of the classic Georgian architecture of the stations being built in the 1930's. (C&O photo CS PR 20190, C&OHS Collection)

Employee Time Tables for 1938

Employee Time Tables of the New River and Alleghany Sub-Division for 1938 are included here.

Many of the train pictures throughout the book show the location, train number and time. The reader may wish to verify this information with the Time Tables, also the class of the train, where it has been and where it is going within the New River and Alleghany Sub-Divisions.

HINTON DIVISION
NEW RIVER SUB-DIVISION
WESTWARD

Calls	Hours Open	Distance from Hinton		STATIONS TIME TABLE No. 130. In Effect Sunday, Feb. 27, 1938.	FIRST CLASS.			
					1 Daily	3 Daily	47 Daily	15 Daily Ex. Sun.
					L AM	L AM	L PM	L PM
HX	Continuous	.0	Wty	HINTON	1 20	7 45	8 18	8 40
CW	Continuous	2.0		C. W. Cabin 2.0	--------	--		
		5.0		R. K. Cabin 3.0				8 48
		9.0		Sandstone 4.0				
MD	Continuous	12.3	W	Meadow Creek 3.3	1 36	s 8 04	8 35	8 57
QN	Continuous	21.7	Wy	Quinnimont 9.4	1 47	8 15	8 47	9 09
NI	Continuous	22.9		Prince 1.2	1 49	8 17	8 50	9 11
		26.2		McKendree 3.3	1 54	8 23	8 56	9 16
CS	Continuous	32.4	t	C. S. Cabin 6.2	2 02	8 31	9 06	9 24
DU	Continuous	33.7	W	Thurmond 1.3 ㉙⑬	2 04	s 8 35	s 9 12	s 9 31
ED	Continuous	40.5	W	Sewell 6.8	2 13	8 45	9 23	9 43
		43.1	W	Keeneys Creek 2.6	2 17	8 49	9 28	9 47
MZ		47.2		Fayette 4.1	2 23	8 55	9 34	9 53
MA	Continuous	51.8		M. A. Cabin 4.6	2 31	9 02	9 42	10 01
GU	Continuous	57.7		G. U. Cabin 5.9	2 40	9 11	9 52	10 11
		57.9		Gauley 0.2				
VN	Continuous	64.2		Deepwater 6.3	2 48	9 19	10 01	10 19
		65.0		West Deepwater 0.8				
		66.6	W	Mt. Carbon 1.6	2 51	9 21	10 04	10 23
CN	8.10 a. m. to 5.10 p. m.	70.4		Montgomery 3.8 ⑬	2 57	s 9 27	s10 12	s10 31
RO	Continuous	72.5	Wt	HANDLEY 2.1	3 02	9 33	10 18	10 38
					A AM	A AM	A PM	A PM
					1 Daily	3 Daily	47 Daily	15 Daily Ex. Sun.

HINTON DIVISION
NEW RIVER SUB-DIVISION
WESTWARD

Distance from Hinton		STATIONS TIME TABLE No. 130. In Effect Sunday, Feb. 27, 1938.	SECOND CLASS.					THIRD CLASS.		
			7 Daily Ex. Sun.	155 Daily	189 Mixed D'y Ex. Sun.	13 Daily	157 Daily Ex. Sun.	93 Daily	99 Daily	95 Daily
			L AM	L AM	L AM	L PM	L PM	L AM	L PM	L PM
.0	Wty	HINTON 2.0	5 30	--------	--------	1 35	--------	--------	--------	--------
2.0		C. W. Cabin 3.0	--------	--------	--------	--------	--------	3 00	2 30	4 30
5.0		R. K. Cabin 4.0	5 39	--------	--------	1 44	--------	3 09	2 40	4 39
9.0		Sandstone 3.3	s 5 48	--------	--------	s 1 53	--------	3 17	2 50	4 48
12.3	W	Meadow Creek 9.4	s 5 57	--------	--------	s 2 01	--------	3 24	2 58	4 56
21.7	Wy	Quinnimont 1.2	s 6 18	7 05	--------	s 2 20	2-30	3 39	3 17	5 15
22.9		Prince 3.3	s 6 22	s 7 09	--------	s 2 25	s 2 34	3 42	3 21	5 19
26.2		McKendree 6.2	f 6 30	--------	--------	f 2 33	--------	3 51	3 30	5 28
32.4	t	C. S. Cabin 1.3	6 45	--------	--------	2 47	--------	4 04	3 40	5 38
33.7	W	Thurmond ㉙⑬ 6.8	s 6 55	--------	--------	s 2 55	--------	4 10	3 50	5 47
40.5	W	Sewell 2.6	s 7 11	--------	11 20	s 3 15	--------	4 25	4 08	6 05
43.1	W	Keeneys Creek 4.1	f 7 18	--------	s11 26	f 3 22	--------	4 31	4 16	6 14
47.2		Fayette 4.6	s 7 26	--------	--------	s 3 31	--------	4 40	4 26	6 23
51.8		M. A. Cabin 5.9	7 35	--------	--------	3 42	--------	4 50	4 36	6 33
57.7		G. U. Cabin 0.2	7 45	--------	--------	3 52	--------	5 06	4 49	6 46
57.9		Gauley 6.3	s 7 46	--------	--------	s 3 55	--------			
64.2		Deepwater 0.8	s 7 57	--------	--------	s 4 08	--------	5 20	5 01	7 01
65.0		West Deepwater 1.6	f 7 59	--------	--------	f 4 12	--------			
66.6	W	Mt. Carbon 3.8	s 8 02	--------	--------	s 4 16	--------	5 24	5 06	7 06
70.4		Montgomery ⑲ 2.1	s 8 13	--------	--------	s 4 27	--------			
72.5	Wt	HANDLEY	s 8 19	--------	--------	s 4 34	--------	5 55	5 30	7 25
			A AM	A AM	A AM	A PM	A PM	A AM	A PM	A PM
			7 Daily Ex. Sun.	155 Daily	189 Mixed D'y Ex. Sun.	13 Daily	157 Daily Ex. Sun.	93 Daily	99 Daily	95 Daily

HINTON DIVISION
NEW RIVER SUB-DIVISION
EASTWARD

Side Track Capacity in Cars (45 ft.)	Distance from Handley		STATIONS	TIME TABLE No. 130. In Effect Sunday, Feb. 27, 1938.	4 Daily Ex. Sun. A AM	44 Sunday Only A AM	16 Daily Ex. Sun. A AM	6 Daily A PM	2 Daily A AM
Yard {	72.5	Wty	HINTON		4 53	5 55	6 35	6 51	12 46
	70.5		C. W. Cabin	2.0	-------	-------	-------	-------	-------
c 61 o 3	67.5		R. K. Cabin	3.0	-------	-------	-------	-------	-------
o 22	63.5		Sandstone	4.0	-------	-------	-------	-------	-------
e 145 w 110 o132	60.2	W	Meadow Creek	3.3	4 39	5 37	s 6 13	6 35	12 30
e 103 w 90 Yard	50.8	Wy	Quinnimont	9.4	4 28	s 5 20	s 5 55	6 22	12 17
o 8	49.6		Prince	1.2	4 26	5 11	5 44	6 19	12 15
c 57 o 35	46.3		McKendree	3.3	4 20	5 05	5 38	6 14	12 10
c 117	40.1	t	C. S. Cabin	6.2	4 12	4 57	5 30	6 06	12 02
e 135 Yard	38.8	W	Thurmond (23)(15)	1.3	4 09	s 4 53	s 5 25	s 6 02	s11 59
Yard	32.0	W	Sewell	6.8	4 00	4 38	5 20	5 50	11 48
e 105 w 149 o11 o36	25.0		South Fayette	7.0	3 50	4 27	4 58	5 40	11 38
--------	20.7		M. A. Cabin	4.3	3 43	4 18	4 50	5 32	11 31
o115	14.8		G. U. Cabin	5.0	3 33	4 09	4 39	5 24	11 21
c 61	14.6		Gauley	0.2	-------	-------	-------	-------	-------
e 103 w 95 Yard	8.3		Deepwater	6.3	3 25	4 00	4 30	5 16	11 12
--------	7.5		West Deepwater	0.8	-------	-------	-------	-------	-------
o 85	5.9	W	Mt. Carbon	1.6	3 22	3 56	4 26	5 13	11 09
o106	2.1		Montgomery (19)	3.8	3 16	s 3 50	s 4 20	s 5 07	s11 04
Yard	.0	Wt	HANDLEY	2.1	3 12	3 45	4 15	5 02	11 00
					L AM	L AM	L AM	L PM	L PM
					4 Daily Ex. Sun.	44 Sunday Only	16 Daily Ex. Sun.	6 Daily	2 Daily

HINTON DIVISION
NEW RIVER SUB-DIVISION
EASTWARD

Distance from Handley		STATIONS	TIME TABLE No. 130. In Effect Sunday, Feb. 27, 1938.	SECOND CLASS				THIRD CLASS		
				156 Daily A AM	14 Daily A PM	158 Daily Ex. Sun. A PM	8 Daily Ex. Sun. A PM	94 Daily A AM	98 Daily A AM	92 Daily A PM
72.5	Wty	HINTON		-------	1 05	-------	6 25	-------	-------	-------
70.5		C. W. Cabin	2.0	-------	-------	-------	-------	5 00	11 30	5 30
67.5		R. K. Cabin	3.0	-------	12 56	-------	6 16	4 45	11 00	5 22
63.5		Sandstone	4.0	-------	s12 46	-------	f 6 08	4 32	10 40	5 12
60.2	W	Meadow Creek	3.3	-------	s12 40	-------	s 6 01	4 25	10 22	5 07
50.8	Wy	Quinnimont	9.4	11 20	s12 17	5 25	s 5 45	4 06	9 45	4 47
49.6		Prince	1.2	11 15	s12 06	5 21	s 5 40	4 02	9 35	4 43
46.3		McKendree	3.3	-------	f11 57	-------	f 5 33	3 54	9 25	4 35
40.1	t	C. S. Cabin	6.2	-------	11 40	-------	5 18	3 39	9 10	4 20
38.8	W	Thurmond (23)(15)	1.3	-------	s11 37	-------	s 5 15	3 35	9 00	4 15
32.0	W	Sewell	6.8	-------	s11 17	-------	s 4 55	3 18	8 40	3 55
25.0		South Fayette	7.0	-------	s10 57	-------	s 4 33	3 02	8 15	3 40
20.7		M. A. Cabin	4.3	-------	10 44	-------	4 20	2 47	7 52	3 25
14.8		G. U. Cabin	5.9	-------	10 33	-------	4 09	2 30	7 36	3 10
14.6		Gauley	0.2	-------	s10 30	-------	f 4 07	-------	-------	-------
8.3		Deepwater	6.3	-------	s10 12	-------	f 3 58	2 18	7 20	2 58
7.5		West Deepwater	0.8	-------	f10 08	-------	-------	-------	-------	-------
5.9	W	Mt. Carbon	1.6	-------	f10 03	-------	f 3 53	2 13	7 10	2 53
2.1		Montgomery (19)	3.8	-------	s 9 56	-------	s 3 45	2 05	7 00	2 45
.0	Wt	HANDLEY	2.1	-------	9 50	-------	3 40	2 00	6 50	2 40
				L AM	L AM	L PM	L PM	L AM	L AM	L PM
				156 Daily	14 Daily	158 Daily Ex. Sun.	8 Daily Ex. Sun.	94 Daily	98 Daily	92 Daily

CLIFTON FORGE DIVISION
ALLEGHANY SUB-DIVISION
WESTWARD

Calls	Hours Open	Distance from Clifton Forge	TIME TABLE No. 130. In Effect Sunday, Feb. 27, 1938. STATIONS.	FIRST CLASS.		
				3 Daily	**47** Daily	**1** Daily
				L AM	L PM	L PM
F	Continuous	.0	Wt **CLIFTON FORGE**	5 10	5 40	11 08
		3.0	H. Y. Cabin			
		1.1				
		4.1	Low Moor	5 17	5 47	11 15
		8.6				
CD	6.45 a. m. to 3.45 p. m.	12.7	Wt Covington	s 5 35	s 6 05	s11 30
		2.2				
BS	Continuous	14.9	W B. S. Cabin	5 39	6 09	11 34
		5.6				
OX	Continuous	20.5	Moss Run	5 50	6 20	11 45
		6.7				
		27.2	Jerrys Run	6 03	6 33	11 58
		2.2				
A	Continuous	29.4	Wt Alleghany	6 07	6 37	12 02
		1.5				
		30.9	Tuckahoe	6 09	6 39	12 04
		3.8				
		34.7	White Sulphur Springs	s 6 20	s 6 50	12 10
		0.4				
WS	Continuous	35.1	W. S. Cabin			
		7.6				
		42.7	Whitcomb	6 32	7 02	12 22
		2.8				
RV	Continuous	45.5	Wt Ronceverte	s 6 43	s 7 13	12 26
		6.5				
		52.0	Fort Spring	6 53	7 23	12 35
		6.8				
		58.8	Alderson ⑲	s 7 05	s 7 35	12 44
		0.5				
AD	Continuous	59.3	W A. D. Cabin			
		11.4				
		70.7	Talcott	7 22	7 52	1 00 [93]
		1.8				
MW	Continuous	72.5	Hilldale	7 25	7 55	1 03
		6.1				
MX	Continuous	78.6	M. X. Cabin			
		1.3				
HX	Continuous	79.9	Wty **HINTON**	7 40 A AM	8 10 A PM	1 15 A AM
				3 Daily	**47** Daily	**1** Daily

CLIFTON FORGE DIVISION
ALLEGHANY SUB-DIVISION
WESTWARD

Distance from Clifton Forge	TIME TABLE No. 130. In Effect Sunday, Feb. 27, 1938. STATIONS.	SECOND CLASS.		THIRD CLASS.	
		13 Daily Ex. Sun.	**143** Daily Ex. Sun.	**95** Daily	**93** Daily
		L AM	L PM	L AM	L PM
.0	Wt **CLIFTON FORGE**	10 30		10 45	10 00
3.0	H. Y. Cabin			10 55	10 10
4.1	Low Moor	s10 39		11 00	10 15
12.7	Wt Covington	s10 55			
14.9	W B. S. Cabin	10 59		11 20	10 36
20.5	Moss Run	f11 11		11 34	10 54
27.2	Jerrys Run	f11 25		11 55	11 16
29.4	Wt Alleghany	s11 31		12 08	11 34
30.9	Tuckahoe	f11 34		12 13	11 39
34.7	White Sulphur Springs	s11 45			
35.1	W. S. Cabin			12 21	11 47
42.7	Whitcomb	f11 59	5 40	12 35	12 01
45.5	Wt Ronceverte	s12 08	5 50	12 43	12 07
52.0	Fort Spring	s12 22		12 55	12 24
58.8	Alderson ⑲	s12 35			
59.3	W A. D. Cabin			1 09	12 39
70.7	Talcott	s 1 05		1 32	1 00 [1]
72.5	Hilldale	f 1 10		1 37	1 10
78.6	M. X. Cabin				
79.9	Wty **HINTON**	1 30 A PM		2 45 A PM	2 00 A AM
		13 Daily Ex. Sun.	**143** Daily Ex. Sun.	**95** Daily	**93** Daily

CLIFTON FORGE DIVISION
ALLEGHANY SUB-DIVISION
EASTWARD

Side Track Capacity in Cars (45 ft.)		Distance from Hinton	STATIONS. TIME TABLE No. 130. In Effect Sunday, Feb. 27, 1938.	2 Daily	4 Daily Ex. Sun.	44 Sun. Only.	6 Daily
				A AM	A AM	A AM	A PM
Yard		79.9	Wt CLIFTON FORGE	2 55	7 10	8 10	9 20
Yard		76.9	H. Y. Cabin	----	----	----	----
	o 78	75.8	Low Moor	2 45	7 03	8 03	9 11
Yard		67.2	Wt Covington	2 32	s 6 50	s 7 50	s 8 58
c 205	o 92	65.0	W B. S. Cabin	2 30	6 45	7 45	8 50
c 108		59.4	Moss Run	2 22	6 37	7 37	8 42
c 114	o 20	52.7	Jerrys Run	2 13	6 28	7 28	8 33
w 155 e 134	o 17	50.5	Wt Alleghany	2 10	6 25	7 25	8 30
c 41	o 6	49.0	Tuckahoe	2 07	6 22	7 22	8 27
	o 48	45.2	White Sulphur Springs	2 00	s 6 15	s 7 15	s 8 20
e 104		44.8	W. S. Cabin				
----		37.2	Whitcomb	1 49	6 00	7 00	7 58
Yard		34.4	Wt Ronceverte	1 45	s 5 55	s 6 55	s 7 53
c 152	o 32	27.9	Fort Spring	1 36	5 42	6 42	7 41
	o 55	21.1	Alderson ⑲	1 25	s 5 30	s 6 30	s 7 30
w 157 e 153	o 21	20.6	W A. D. Cabin	----	----	----	----
c 93	o 35	9.2	Talcott	1 10	5 15	6 15	7 15
	o 27	7.4	Hilldale	1 07	5 12	6 12	7 12
		1.3	M. X. Cabin	----	----	----	----
Yard		.0	Wty HINTON	12 55 L AM	5 00 L AM	6 00 L AM ⁹⁴	7 00 L PM
				2 Daily	4 Daily Ex. Sun.	44 Sun. Only	6 Daily

CLIFTON FORGE DIVISION
ALLEGHANY SUB-DIVISION
EASTWARD

Distance from Hinton	STATIONS. TIME TABLE No. 130. In Effect Sunday, Feb. 27, 1938.	SECOND CLASS.		THIRD CLASS.		
		16 Daily Ex. Sun.	142 Daily Ex. Sun.	94 Daily	98 Daily	92 Daily
		A AM	A AM	A AM	A PM	A PM
79.9	Wt CLIFTON FORGE	9 40	----	10 30	6 00	11 30
76.9	H. Y. Cabin	----	----	9 58	5 30	11 05
75.8	Low Moor	f 9 26	----	9 47	5 27	11 02
67.2	Wt Covington	s 9 08	----			
65.0	W B. S. Cabin	8 59	----	9 24	4 53	10 32
59.4	Moss Run	f 8 47	----	9 03	4 32	10 11
52.7	Jerrys Run	f 8 36	----	8 40	4 09	9 48
50.5	Wt Alleghany	s 8 31 ⁹⁴	----	8 31 ¹⁶	3 53	9 42
49.0	Tuckahoe	f 8 28	----	8 10	3 48	9 37
45.2	White Sulphur Springs	s 8 20	----			
44.8	W. S. Cabin	----	----	7 55	3 33	9 22
37.2	Whitcomb	f 8 04	f 8 11	7 27	3 05	8 57
34.4	Wt Ronceverte	s 7 58	8 05	7 20	2 58	8 50
27.9	Fort Spring	s 7 43		7 05	2 45	8 35
21.1	Alderson ⑲	s 7 29				
20.6	W A. D. Cabin	----	----	6 50	2 30	8 22
9.2	Talcott	s 7 03		6 27	2 07	8 00
7.4	Hilldale	f 6 58		6 15	1 55	7 55
1.3	M. X. Cabin	----	----			
.0	Wty HINTON	6 45 L AM	---- L AM	6 00 L AM ⁴⁴	1 30 L PM	7 30 L PM
		16 Daily Ex. Sun.	142 Daily Ex. Sun.	94 Daily	98 Daily	92 Daily

Hawks Nest, the C&O bridge across the New River at Hawks Nest. The double tracks of the C&O east bound are approaching the bridges from the right side of the picture. The east bound track continues on the right side of the river. The west bound track crosses the bridge and continues on the left (south) side of the river. The curve from the end of the bridges to the south side of the river is the sharpest (15° degrees) on the entire railway; trains were limited to 15 miles per hour. (Postcard)

As we looked across the river we are just able to catch a glimpse of a west bound train of empty hopper cars coming off the bridge with an H-7 (2-8-8-2) at the head. (Rob Downey)

Chapter I

THE NEW RIVER GORGE AND THE KAYMOOR COAL MINE

The New River would be more aptly named "The Old River." It is perhaps the oldest river in North America, tracing its ancestry back two million years from its headwaters in North Carolina. It followed its parent, the Teays River, on its course through present day West Virginia. Accordingly it is the New River that gave the C&O Railway its passage through the rugged Appalachian Mountains.

In 1869 the Chesapeake & Ohio Railway surveyed the New River Gorge for a route west to the Ohio River. Construction crews worked in both directions from Hinton in the east and Huntington in the west. The two crews met about one mile east of Hawks Nest on January 29, 1873, completing the railway.

Traveling from west to east, the New River Gorge begins at Hawks Nest. The entire mainline of the C&O is double track. However, at this point the "V" shaped canyon walls are so steep that there was not room for two tracks on either side of the river. As a result, the railway had to split the tracks; the eastbound track remained on the south side of the river, and the west bound track crossed the river to the north side.
We are traveling eastward in the summer of 1938. There are many coal mine tipples on each side of the river, because the Sewell coal seam had out cropping high on both sides of the walls. The Sewell coal seam is 560 feet above the New River at Kaymoor.

The first coal shipment from Kaymoor was August 23, 1900 and was on a C&O hopper car. Mine operators always named their mines. Kaymoor was named after superintendent James Kay. There is a town at the top on the rim of the gorge and one at the bottom by the C&O tracks. In 1925 the highly productive and profitable Kaymoor mine was sold to the Berwind New River Pocahontas Company for $1,001,000. At the time Kaymoor became one of the 19 coal mines owned by Berwind in West Virginia (they also owned mines in Pennsylvania, Kentucky and Virginia.) This huge company was shipping coal east and north to utilities in the east, and under contract supplied the coal for the U.S. Navy. They owned a fleet of their own hopper cars for this purpose. In fact, virtually all of the hopper cars at this time were either C&O cars or Berwind cars.

As we approach the Kaymoor facilities, we see the old stone powerhouse. This powerhouse ceased operating in 1925 when reliable public electricity became available. Just beyond the powerhouse are the tipples. The coal tipples screen and grade coal from four-inch size to slack and pulverized slacks. The slack coal was used for making coke. The graded coal, from lump, eggs and nut sizes, is shipped to the coal markets.

Old Kaymoor stone powerhouse, now abandoned. Power is now being purchased from a public utility company. (Bernard Kempinski)

Engine H-4 (2-6-6-2) No. 1367 has arrived at the large Kaymoor mine tipple and dropped empty Berwind hoppers on the main-line while it has pulled in the tipple sidings to begin removing loaded hoppers. (Bernard Kempinski)

This engine has re-entered another siding track to bring in empties. (Bernard Kempinski)

After discharging empty cars it has again moved over on the first siding to pull out another string of loaded hoppers. (Bernard Kempinski)

Chapter II

SEWELL - AN OSHA NIGHTMARE*

Sewell was the first community founded deep in the New River Gorge. The name Sewell comes from Stephan Sewell from New England when he first arrived here in 1749. The huge deposits of high quality coal later named the Sewell Coal Steam that brought great commercial activity to this region were unknown to him. The Town of Sewell owes its existence solely to its location as a receiving point for shipping out this coal and also for converting a portion of it into coke.

In earlier days charcoal was used in the production of iron, but sources of wood for charcoal were quickly depleted. It was discovered that coke was better than coal to make iron and later steel. Coke is produced from coal by heating the coal, but allowing only a reduced supply of air. As a result, coke burns hotter and cleaner than coal and became the standard fuel of the iron and steel mills of the nation.

In this area, the most productive coalmines were at the top of the high cliffs overlooking Mann's Creek Canyon.

Mann's Creek Canyon was a steep-walled gorge running out of the New River Gorge. Dense virgin timber and rock outcropping lined the walls. It was considered almost impassable. But the coal was on top of the gorge and the railway was at the bottom. After first being told that a railroad could not be built in this steep gorge, another engineer said it could be done. It required that a narrow gage railroad of 36-inch track width would have to run around all the bluffs and up all the ravines in order to get the distance required to raise the elevation of more than 1,200 feet from the railway by the New River up to the top of the cliff. This still resulted in grades from 3% to 6%. The resulting treacherous railway was 8 1/2 miles long and became the Mann's Creek Railway.

With the completion of the Mann's Creek Railway, the future of Sewell seemed assured. Many houses were built including the red row houses between the railway tracks and the New River. Stores, schools and churches were built. The C&O erected a passenger station with a hexangular tower on the roof for the telegraph operator. A freight station was also built across the tracks.

Several local passenger trains served the town daily.

In 1938 there are miles and miles of coke ovens along the C&O mainline through the New River Gorge. At night these coke ovens cast a red glow along the entire railway that could be seen for miles.

*OSHA – Occupational Safety and Health Administration (a U.S. Government bureau to protect the health and safety of workers – unknown in 1938). *See page 19; bottom two pictures.*

Our afternoon train #6, the FFV headed by one of those beautiful polished Pacific (4-6-2), is just crossing over the New River Bridge on its approach to Sewell. (Bernard Kempinski)

Another quick view of the FFV. (Bernard Kempinski)

We turn around quickly to see the Sewell station, the coke ovens with the black laborers' houses on the hillside above the coke ovens. (Bernard Kempinski)

The actual Sewell station with a speeder across the tracks. (C&OHS)

Model of Sewell station with a speeder across the tracks. (Bernard Kempinski)

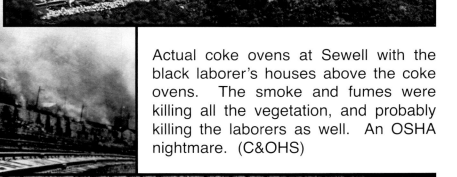

Actual coke ovens at Sewell with the black laborer's houses above the coke ovens. The smoke and fumes were killing all the vegetation, and probably killing the laborers as well. An OSHA nightmare. (C&OHS)

Model of coke ovens and black laborers' homes on hillside above coke ovens. (Bernard Kempinski)

The FFV is leaving Sewell and is following the New River on the way to Thurmond. (Rob Downey)

The FFV continues along the New River on its way to Thurmond. (Bernard Kempinski)

We now have some time to see Sewell. The first thing we want to see is the Mann's Creek Railway. We found their engine No. 5 pushing some of these unique homemade hopper cars into the head house. In 1938 the Mann's Creek Railway possessed the following engines: Climax No. 3, Climax No. 4, Climax No. 6, Shay No. 8 (the only engine ever bought new), Shay No. 2 and the second No. 5, pictured here in Sewell. This Shay is two trucks, 36 ton with 3 cylinders. It was built in 1926 for the Wilderness Lumber Company of West Virginia and was the last engine purchased (in 1938) by the Mann's Creek Railway. (Bernard Kempinski)

A bit later in the afternoon Shay No. 5 has returned to the stone engine house. (Bernard Kempinski)

Actual Mann's Creek engine house. Note the track going down to C&O Mainline. (C&OHS)

Model of Mann's Creek engine house, with track going down to C&O Mainline. (Rob Downey)

Here are the coke ovens at Sewell, stretching alongside the C&O Railway mainline for nearly a mile. The smoke and fumes from the coke ovens went 24 hours per day. Seen above the ovens through the smoke are the homes of the black laborers. You can see the smoke and fumes have killed all of the vegetation around the ovens. It is probably killing the laborers as well. (C&OHS)

Our model of the same scene shows the black laborers' homes and dying vegetation.

Actual view showing pulling coke from one of the ovens. (C&OHS)

Same view as modeled. Why coke? Coke is produced from coal by heating it but restricting the amount of air allowed so it does not actually burn. Coke with higher carbon content burns hotter than coal. This is a big advantage in making steel. (Rob Downey)

Engine 1397 (2-6-6-2) left its hoppers to run down to the water tank on the west end of Sewell. (Bernard Kempinski)

As we look across the bend in the river, we see a westbound empty hopper train approaching, headed by a 2-8-8-2 engine. (Bernard Kempinski)

Now coming down the middle of Sewell, we see the freight station, the great Eastern Bargain House and the red row houses on the right. (Bernard Kempinski)

As we track its progress, the coke ovens and tipple come into view. (Bernard Kempinski)

The caboose has just passed the Great Eastern Bargain House. (Bernard Kempinski)

In case you don't believe this "wild" looking building, here is a picture of the real Great Eastern Bargain House. This was an independent store. Sewell also had its company store (with higher prices), but took the miners' script, which could not be used elsewhere. (C&OHS)

With the westbound mainline hopper train now gone, the crew on engine 1397 has returned from the water tank to pull out the loaded hopper cars in the siding by the coke ovens. (Bernard Kempinski)

The loaded hoppers have been set out on the mainline while string of empty hoppers are being pushed into the siding (Bernard Kempinski)

The crew of engine 1397 has returned to the main-line, picked up the loaded hopper cars and proceeded westbound. To their right we see the superintendent's house and the Sewell station just beyond. (Bernard Kempinski)

The caboose of the local mine turn is just passing the Sewell station as its proceeds westward on the single north side track approaching the New River Gorge. (Bernard Kempinski)

Chapter III

THURMOND - "HELL WITH A RIVER RUNNING THROUGH IT"

Thurmond is in the heart of West Virginia's New River Gorge. Captain William Thurmond and the C&O Railway appeared at the location within a few months of each other in 1873. Like most of the New River Gorge, this area has steep hills on both sides. It also was the site of two creeks opening into the New River. This made a natural route into the Gorge which became very important in bringing in coal from a large surrounding area. Thurmond noted this and acquired this area in return for surveying he had done. He was right; with the arrival of the C&O and the passage of 30 years, Thurmond became a major shipping point. In some years it supplied more than twice the freight tonnage and revenue of Cincinnati and Richmond, Virginia combined!

William Thurmond was an upright Baptist, unaccepting of weakness or vice in himself or others. So how did the town of Thurmond get such an awful reputation?

The town of Thurmond was strictly governed. What an irony that it received its reputation of hard drinking, gambling and prostitution from the surrounding communities, particularly Glen Jean across the river. This town was located on some 25,000 acres owned by Mr. William McKell, and it even extended across the New River and bordered the much smaller acreage of Thurmond. It was not easily perceived where one jurisdiction ended and the other began. This was the problem.

McKell had no strong feelings against drinking, gambling and even prostitution. After long, hard days in the coal mines, it was easy to see that this was the place to blow off steam and the paycheck with drinking, gambling and other vices. Even though this was centered across the river at McKell's Dun Glen Hotel and at the more unsavory establishments that sprang up around it, it was Thurmond that got the reputation, to the deep chagrin of Captain Thurmond. As usual, crime accompanied this raucous activity; scarcely a week went by without at least one shooting. (The New River was a handy place to dispose of the body.)

The Dun Glen Hotel had its share of noteworthy events. It was reported by Ripley's Believe It or Not that the hotel hosted a poker game that ran continuously for 14 years and that the bar never closed. The Dun Glen was the place for the big business deals to be made. It was here that Paddy Rand made his million dollar deal with Edward Berwind for the Minden mines.

As the story goes, Rand was so elated with the deal he bought drinks for everyone at the bar, boarded the next outbound train, and was never seen again.

The first loads of coal arrived in Thurmond in 1889. This was the beginning of Thurmond's boom era. By 1898 Thurmond had a population of 175 people. During the next few years over thirty homes were built. There was a Western Union, Adams Express, two general stores, offices of two coal companies, a drug store, restaurant, saloon, lawyer, two milliners, wholesale distributor, shoemaker, jeweler and a photographer. The original hotel to the west of the National Bank of Thurmond burned in 1899. It was replaced in 1902 by the three-story, thirty-five room Hotel Thurmond. The Armour meat processing plant is to the immediate west of the Hotel Thurmond.

The Mankin-Cox Building, the eastern most structure, was built in 1904. The Goodwin-Kincaid Building (to the immediate west of the Mankin-Cox Building) was built in 1906. In 1917 the four story brick building housing the National Bank of Thurmond was built.

Thurmond is first and foremost a railroad town. In fact, it has no main street! The double track mainline left no room for a street. The railway yards are between the mainline tracks and the New River. The only place left for these commercial buildings was between the railroad tracks and the steep hillside behind the buildings.

The Thurmond railway yard underwent a major expansion after 1902. Also in 1902, the passenger station burned. In 1904 the present passenger station was under construction. It was necessary to provide the many offices in the station to accommodate the large volume of traffic originating in Thurmond. In 1904 Thurmond produced one-fourth of the entire C&O revenue. As many as 200 railroaders worked in Thurmond on three eight-hour shifts.

In 1910 Thurmond produced $4,878,607 in freight and passenger revenues. By contrast Cincinnati's total revenue that year was $1,816,392. The third city, Richmond, Virginia, earned less that $500,000. The entire C&O Railway that year earned $24,901,200 in revenues, and the Hinton Division accounted for $10,896,769 of that total. Clearly, New River coal was the lifeblood of the Chesapeake and Ohio Railway, and Thurmond was the heart which kept it pumping.

Between 1910 and 1930 railroad activity at Thurmond was at its peak. More structures were added to the yards: two new water storage tanks and bunkhouse for train men. In 1921 the engine house was enlarged to serve four Mallet (2-6-6-2) engines at one time. In 1922 the huge Fairbanks-Morse concrete coaling station was constructed. It was designed to service two yard tracks and two mainline tracks. Incoming coal was brought in on the center track under the structure. Thurmond was the home of over 30 steam engines, comprised principally of Consolidations (2-8-0) and Mallets (2-6-6-2). None of these 2-6-6-2 Mallets operated on the mainline; they and the

Consolidations were found to be ideal for the many mine runs out of Thurmond. The loaded coal cars at Thurmond are picked up and empty cars dropped off by larger 2-8-8-2 articulated engines.

By 1938 the booming days of Thurmond were ending, and it had settled down to become a quiet town. The Dun Glen Hotel across the river was destroyed by fire in 1930. There is still a great deal of coal being shipped from Thurmond, but most of the surrounding mines are now in decline.

"A one-way ticket to... Hell!"

In 1887 the fare was fifty cents ... the destination—Coal Valley, West Virginia. Here's how the old-timers tell the story:

It was a Saturday night back in 1887. Thurmond on the New River was full of rollicking miners from the hills. As it got close to midnight, one hard-bitten case rolled into the C & O Railway station:

"Where you going?" asked the agent.

"I'm going to hell!" roared the miner.

"Coal Valley, eh? That'll be fifty cents."

Coal Valley was a wild and woolly place in those days. It was filled with the raw, restless spirit that was building America ... literally from scratch. Like Abilene, Dodge City, Tombstone, and other famous mining towns, it was the source of our nation's wealth. For coal was to be the powerful right arm of American industry.

Here again, it was the railroad that channeled this raw power to the nerve centers; the steel mills, the factories and homes in spreading metropolitan areas. And as the coal rolled out, a wave of reform swept in along the shining rails of the C & O. Churches, schools and hospitals were built. Banks opened and small businesses thrived.

An era had begun. An era that was to open the richest coal producing fields in the world. Today, in the Chessie Corridor, hundreds of modern cities and towns stand as monuments to the progressive leadership of the coal industry and the C & O.

The FFV has just rounded the curve leading into Thurmond. On the left is the giant coaling tower, servicing four tracks, two on the yard side and two on the mainline. On the right is the Thurmond Hotel with the Armour packing house behind it. (Bernard Kempinski)

The FFV is approaching closer. As can be seen the main street of Thurmond has space for only the two mainline tracks of the C & O. No room for a street or cars. (Bernard Kempinski)

We can now see the engine house in the yards.
(Bernard Kempinski)

As the FFV continues down "main street," the
Mankin building is in the foreground with several
stores beyond. (Bernard Kempinski)

Pacific 474 under the cantilever signal bridge. (Bernard Kempinski)

We have a meet right on the "main street" of Thurmond with an articulated 2-8-8-2 leading a westbound string of empty hoppers. (Bernard Kempinski)

The engine of the FFV is just coming to a stop beyond the Thurmond depot. (Bernard Kempinski)

We have taken a walk over to the Thurmond yard just in time to see engine 1397 arriving with a string of loaded hoppers from its mine run to Sewell. Consolidated (2-8-0) is just pulling out of the engine house. (Bernard Kempinski)

Engine 1397 has dropped off the loaded hoppers to be picked up later by a mainline H-7 (2-8-8-2) and taken to Hinton on their first stop east. It has now moved to the coaling tower. (Bernard Kempinski)

The Thurmond engine house is always a busy place. It can accommodate six engines at a time. Smoke stack in fore-ground is the boiler, creating steam and heat for the engine house and the Thurmond station. (Bernard Kempinski)

Berwind hopper cars are marked "When empty return to Thurmond, C&O Ry." (Bernard Kempinski)

With a lull in the yard activity, I crossed the tracks to take a picture of the Hotel Thurmond. The National Bank of Thurmond is to the right, Armour packing house to the left. (Bernard Kempinski)

A few minutes later a merchandise express headed by No. 1231 Mikado (2-8-2) comes rushing through with bell ringing (at 20 MPH) the speed limit through Thurmond. The C & O commissary is in the background. (Bernard Kempinski)

Finally, here is a picture of the actual Thurmond Station with an Elite Laundry truck alongside. (C & O HS)

The model of same. (Rob Downey)

The Thurmond station seen from the road across the tracks. (C & O HS)

The model of same. (Rob Downey)

The model of the coaling tower at Thurmond. (Rob Downey)

The actual coaling tower at Thurmond. (C & O HS)

Rear of the Thurmond station. (Rob Downey)

Chapter IV

QUINNIMONT, PRINCE AND FANNY

QUINNIMONT

In Latin, Quinnimont means five mountains, and so it is. Quinnimont is located at the junction of Laurel Creek and the New River. It is one of the very few places on the entire length of the New River that has enough level land wide enough to construct a railway wye. This is where the Laurel Creek branch heads east up its namesake stream's valley' 6 miles to five coal mines, terminating at Layland. As with many other branches on the C & 0, the Laurel Creek branch is on a steep grade, at some points 3.8%.

Quinnimont was the earliest development on the New River, the site of a pig-iron furnace.

The yards in the wye at Quinnimont are not only a collection point for the mines on the Laurel Creek Branch, but also for the far more important Piney Creek Subdivision that extended south at Prince, a mile to the west.

In addition to the considerable movement of hopper cars up and down the branch, there is a daily passenger train for the convenience of the many miners and their families. This train is headed by a Consolidation (2-8-0), with a baggage combine and a passenger coach. It is scheduled to meet mainline local # 13 at the Quinnnimont station.

From Quinnimont to Prince is only 1.3 miles, but these two locations serve entirely different functions. As we have seen, Quinnimont was important for its wye and access to the coal mines up Laurel Creek. Prince became important as a gateway to the city of Beckley, up on top of the plateau.

Overview of Quinnimont showing passenger station foreground, express building behind. Work crew houses across the track. (C & O HS)

A mine run brings a string of empty hoppers into the wye at Quinnimont. To the right is the unique Quinnimont yard office with the interlocking cabin on the roof. (Bernard Kempinski)

Having dropped off the empty hoppers, the Mallet pulls out of the wye to its caboose. To the left of the engine is the express house; behind the engine is the freight house, water tower and pump house for the water tower. (Bernard Kempinski)

The Mallet (2-6-6-2) enters the mainline past the yard office, protected by the cantilever signal. (Bernard Kempinski)

It's 2:00 PM. The Laurel Creek local passenger train is just coming into view around the hillside as it drifts down the branch line to the wye at Quinnimont. (Bernard Kempinski)

The train is taking the right side of the wye. (Bernard Kempinski)

The Laurel Creek local is headed by its usual Consolidation engine (2-8-0) No. 1028. A combine and a coach follow. Here it is passing the Quinnimont water tower. The roof of the freight station can be seen over the tender. In the foreground is one of the five laborer's houses across the mainline (Bernard Kempinski)

Now our local is entering the mainline side of the wye. In the foreground is the bridge over the Laurel Creek. The cantilever signal bridge is in the foreground and the train order signed by the yard office is to the extreme right. In the background is the express building. To the right of the locomotive is the pump shed for the water tower. (Bernard Kempinski)

Our local is backing on the mainline past the express building. (Bernard Kempinski)

The Laurel Creek local is backing to the switch on the other side of the wye. It will pull forward through the switch onto the side of the wye in front of the passenger station. There its passengers will debark to wait for the mainline local, and our Laurel Creek local will wait to take passengers off of the mainline up to the branch (Bernard Kempinski)

It's 2:20 PM; Westbound local #13 is arriving right on time at the Quinnimont station (behind the engine) (Bernard Kempinski)

Passengers have gotten off and boarded the mainline local, which has departed. The passengers that have gotten off the mainline local are now walking over to board the Laurel Creek local to return to their homes up the Laurel Creek branch. (Bernard Kempinski)

Actual passenger station, express
building behind. (C & O HS)

Model of passenger station, express
building behind. (Bernard Kempinski)

Quinnimont yard office with operator's cabin
on roof (C & O HS)

Model of yard office with operator's cabin on roof
(Bernard Kempinski)

PRINCE

The creation of the town of Prince goes back to 1870, three years before the Chesapeake & Ohio Railway arrived here in 1873. The town's creation can be attributed to Mr. William "Bub" Prince, who was the successful owner of a general store in Beckley, W. Va. It is about 18 miles from Beckley to the area that "Bub" Prince thought would be the most likely spot for a railway station. This is where the Piney Creek joined the New River. Bub and his brother, James Prince Sr., after a hard scouting expedition, laid their claim to several hundred acres, which would become Prince and Quinnimont.

In 1873 Bub moved his family and all their possessions from Beckley on top of the mountain down to his site of Prince, where they lived in tents. There were no roads or trails. But with the arrival of the railway, roads were built, goods began to flow. Prince was born. The C & O built the first station at Prince in 1880 with Bub donning the first station agent's cap. The original station was enlarged in 1891, but burned down in 1917. It was quickly rebuilt in 1917 and served Prince in the summer of 1938.

Prince became an important access for passengers in Beckely to reach the outside world via the C & O, which ran down through the New River Gorge. To accomplish this a branch line was built from Prince to Beckley, known as the Piney Creek Branch. There is a passenger train making two round trips each day except Sunday. The morning train meets the mainline local #17 out of Hinton. The afternoon train meets local #13 that also meets the Quinnimont branch train. The Piney Creek branch train took on the affectionate name known to all as "Fanny." It is composed of a Consolidation engine (Class-G-7 or G-9), one express car, a combination baggage and U.S. Mail car, and two-day coaches. Freight cars are attached to the rear of the train as needed.

Local eastbound mainline passenger train number 14, on the way to Prince and Quinnimont, entering Stretcher Neck Tunnel. The train will arrive in a few minutes at Prince at 12:06 PM. Quinnimont is only one mile from Prince; the train is due there at 12:17 PM. (Bernard Kempinski)

Our local is just passing N.I. Cabin before arriving at the Prince station. (Bernard Kempinski)

Actual Prince station and NI Cabin. (C & O HS)

Prince station, with a goodly number of persons ready to board the approaching mainline local. These passengers have come down to Prince from Beckley on "Fanny", their own local for the 18 miles from Beckley to Prince to reach the C & O mainline and the Outside world. (Bernard Kempinski)

After leaving Prince and Quinnimont on the way to Hinton, we round the big 180 degree bend in the New River, with the C & O mainline following the river as seen from Grandview State Park. (C & O HS)

The model of the same. (Rob Downey)

An H-7 Articulated (2-8-8-2) heading a coal drag around the big Grandview curve. (Bernard Kempinski)

Chapter V

HINTON - THE HEARTBEAT OF IT ALL

Hinton was laid out on the land of Avis Gwinn Hinton by her husband, John Hinton, in 1831. The town grew very slowly until 1871, when the Chesapeake & Ohio Railway blasted a path through the New River gorge-and made Hinton the division terminal. The town then started to grow, was incorporated on September 21, 1880. Some historians claim that the town was named for Evan Hinton, who was active in the movement to create Summers County. Others suggest that it was named for John (Jack) Hinton, who was a prominent lawyer in the county and who laid out the town in 1831. In 1927, the towns of Avis, Bellepoint and Hinton were consolidated and incorporated as the city of Hinton by the West Virginia state legislature.

In 1938 Hinton is one of the C & O's busiest terminals. In addition to being a crew change point for all passenger and freight trains, Hinton originates eastbound coal extras, local passenger trains and local freight trains. All of these operations require many engine changes. On the New River, the level Subdivision, passenger trains use Pacifics 4-6-2s, freight trains use Mikados, 2-8-2s, and coal trains use Articulated 2-8-8-2s. Local freight trains could use a Consolidated 2-8-0 or a Mikado 2-8-2.

On the Alleghany Mountain Subdivision, passenger trains use Mountain 4-8-2 or the new Greenbrier 4-8-4 engines. Passenger trains with more than 12 heavyweight cars are double headed. Freight trains all use Articulated 2-8-8-2s, and eastbound loaded coal trains also have a 2-8-8-2 pusher on the rear.

The yards are worked by 0-8-0 and 0-10-0 switches with crews 24 hours per day at both the east and west end.

Even in the days of advanced steam engine technology, steam engines have to be checked and serviced every 100 to 150 miles. Hinton is primarily an engine facility. However, cars are dropped off and picked up by the manifest fast freights for locals to deliver to the stations on the New River and Alleghany Subdivisions as well as the city of Hinton. Huge amounts of coal, sand and other supplies are used in the Hinton yards, as well as loads of cinders to be taken out.

CW Cabin controls the western approach to the Hinton yards. Here we see a westbound empty hopper train snaking out of the yard onto the mainline. The cabin operator is at the bottom of the steps to check the train as it goes by. (Paul Dolkos)

Our train is headed by an H-7 Articulated (2-8-8-2), which is standard heavy freight power in 1938. Note the phone box in front of the signal and the train order signal behind the engine. (Paul Dolkos)

We have a meet coming up. An eastbound loaded hopper train, again powered by an H-7 (2-8-8-2), will proceed past the Hinton yards to the Avis yard to the east of Hinton to pick up a fresh H-7 head engine and a pusher H-7 for the climb over the Allegany Subdivision to Alleghany. (Paul Dolkos)

As the caboose of the westbound empty hopper train passes CW Cabin, the Eastbound loaded hopper train does not stop, because of the difficulty of getting started again on the grade at Hinton. It will go on to the Avis yard, east of Hinton, to change engines and crews and pick up its pusher engine for the climb over the Alleghany Subdivision to Alleghany. Switch Engine (0-8-0) number 175 is resting at the end of its western switch lead track. (Paul Dolkos)

A view of the New River. The giant coaling tower in the Hinton yards can be seen from the eastbound FFV as it rounds the curve approaching Hinton. (Rob Downey)

As we arrive at Hinton, a westbound freight manifest has just come off the Alleghany Subdivision and entered the yards. It is headed by a big H-7 1588 articulated (2-8-8-2.) (Paul Dolkos)

The manifest stopped wit the engine in front of th Hinton station. The roa crew goes off duty at the sta tion and a hostler takes th train to a stop on arrival trac number 1. Switch engine 23 quickly pulls up behind t take off the caboose. Eve engine and train cre changes at Hinton. Th caboose "belongs" to its cor ductor and will not be use on the train when it is reac to depart down the Ne River Subdivision. (Pa Dolkos)

Switch engine 175 has taken a Milwaukee Road box car out of the train. It is consigned to Hinton. (Paul Dolkos)

Engine 175 can be seen pushing the Milwaukee box car up the steep grade from the Hinton yards to the Hinton freight station. The Hinton turntable and several service sheds are in the foreground. (Paul Dolkos)

The switch engine and box car are just arriving at the Hinton freight station. A Railway Express truck waits by the side door. The large building next to the freight station is a warehouse. The building on top of the hill to the left in the picture is an Armour meat-packing house. (Paul Dolkos)

Our manifest has been in the Hinton yards just one hour. In addition to the box car set out for Hinton, there have been a number of westbound cars that have come in from the locals that have gathered them from local towns in the area. Also dropped off in the Hinton yards are cars to be delivered by local freight trains to small towns in the area. This is done so that the through mainline manifest can make much faster time by not stopping with all of these set-outs and pick-ups. By one stop at a division point such as Hinton this is accomplished. Local freight out of Hinton will go east and west for the various set-outs and pick-ups in the New River and Alleghany Subdivisions. These locals will bring the cars back to Hinton for the next through manifests. The big articulated engine 1588 that brought the manifest over the Alleghany Subdivision has been taken off and switched over to the servicing area. A Mikado (2-8-2) number 1231 is now in charge as the train is ready to depart on the more level New River Subdivision on yard track number one. The double track mainline is in the foreground. (Bernard Kempinski)

We will follow engine 1588 as it is checked and serviced in the yard at Hinton. The first stop is the inspection pits. This is the dirtiest job in the yards. Everything is checked and minor repairs are made. If more major repairs are needed, a note is sent in a vacuum tube that connects the inspection pits to the roundhouse. (Bernard Kempinski)

A better view of the inspection pits is seen from the picture taken from up on the coaling tower. The weighing scales can be seen behind engine 1588. (Bernard Kempinski)

Our engine has now moved up to the water plug by the coaling tower, and the tender is going to be topped off. (Bernard Kempinski)

The engine is pulling forward to align with the sand pipes, which are connected to the bottom of the two large vertical bins. (Bernard Kempinski)

Our yard hand has the sand pipe in his right hand and is ready to begin filling the sand domes on top of the engine. (Bernard Kempinski)

The engine is now moved further forward to bring the tender under the coal chutes under the tower. (The coal chutes can be seen hanging down slightly below the underside of the ceiling.) (Paul Dolkos)

Our engine has now moved to the Fairbanks-Morse cinder conveyors to drop the ashes and cinders from the firebox. A conveyor brings the ashes up and over the track behind the engines and dumps them into a designated hopper to be used as fill along the railway. Behind the left conveyor is the sand drying facility. The water tank is to supply the numerous water standpipes throughout the yards. (Bernard Kempinski)

The engine is now moving toward the wash rack. The icing facility can be seen behind the engine. In front of the engine is an old Robertson ash conveyor no longer in use. On top of the hill can be seen a number of the houses on Front Street in Hinton. They actually have a nice river view (with the railway yards and plenty of smoke in between.) (Bernard Kempinski)

We are now on the wash rack. The drivers are washed with hot water and detergent. (Bernard Kempinski)

With the washing completed, our engine is pulling onto the turntable. (Bernard Kempinski)

The engine is being turned to align up with the tracks going to the Mallet House. The east yard switchman's shanty is to the left of the picture. The roundhouse is on the right. (Bernard Kempinski)

Engine 1588 has entered the Mallet house for some routine maintenance. (Bernard Kempinski)

Our engine is pulling off the turntable, proceeding along side of the roundhouse on the way to the Mallet house. (Bernard Kempinski)

Since we have some time, we decided to walk west through the yards. As we go back past the roundhouse, a Mikado (2-8-2) number 2320 has turned on the turntable and is heading out to a westbound ready truck. These Mikes are the workhorses of the C & O; very few get the white striping and the white tires on the drivers. Behind the roundhouse can be seen part of the tall chimney of the power plant. (Bernard Kempinski).

A look back gives us a partial view of the roundhouse. On the extreme right side of the picture you can see the grey wooden roof extension. Since the roundhouse is back against a steep hill, this is an attempt to give more depth to the stalls to accommodate the ever-larger engines. (Bernard Kempinski)

This ice house at the Hinton yards was originally serviced by trucks that loaded ice into the top of the ice house. After 1935 ice was brought in by box cars and loaded into the lower level. This supplied ice for passenger car bunkers as air conditioning of passenger cars was starting. Ice was also used for engine, caboose and yard crews. With this small ice house and short platform no significant icing of through reefers would be practical. However, in the picture, we do have two reefers, originating in Hinton, that are being iced prior to departure. (Bernard Kempinski)

The second view of the icing facilities shows the additional sheds that were added under the overhead platforms to accept ice brought in by rail. (Bernard Kempinski)

Here is another view of the Fairbanks-Morse cinder conveyors. The cinders are picked up by a conveyor under the engine, lifted up and over the adjoining truck and dumped into a hopper car for disposal. (Rob Downey)

The actual cinder conveyors at Hinton. (C & O HS)

We've walked over to get another view of the giant 800-ton coal dock. To the left is the coal dump under the track to receive coal. The coal is brought up in the enclosed conveyor to the top of the dock. The coal drops down into four compartments by separate grade. The older hand-fired engines use a larger lump size than the bigger stoker fed engines. Beyond the coal dump is the sand-drying facility. The dry sand is blown by compressed air to the sand bunkers on the other side of the tower. The inspection pits are in the foreground. (Rob Downey)

Here is the actual coal dock at Hinton. (C & O HS)

This is the famous or infamous Grand Central. No one seems to know its origin. It does not look like a prototypical C & O building, yet it seems to be rather large to be built by the yard employees. (The yard employees did build the east yard switchman shanty). It is located at the west end of the yards for the "comfort" of the switching crews. (Paul Dolkos)

In case you don't believe the model, here are the only known pictures of the real Grand Central, taken by Jim EuDaly. At the time of these pictures, Grand Central had been unused for many years, due to the advent of diesels. It did not appear on early Hinton yard maps, but some later maps actually referred to "Grand Central." (James EuDaly)

A view from the other side of Grand Central Yard Office.(7-21-1970 by Jim EuDaly)

As we walk back towards the eastern side of the yards, we catch H-7 number 1556 (2-8-8-2) just leaving the yards with an eastbound manifest freight. (Bernard Kempinski)

Here is the real Hinton station. (Dan Zugelter)

Here is the model of the Hinton station in 1938. It was a very busy place. The first floor was for baggage and express on the west side; tickets and waiting room were on the east side. The bay window on the second floor was the dispatcher. Among his many duties he had to regulate the heavy traffic on the grade up to Alleghany to keep the slow coal drags moving without slowing the passenger trains or manifest freights. The roof of the YMCA can be seen behind the station. (Rob Downey)

It's 6:51 pm, there are long shadows as the eastbound FFV (No.6) arrives at the Hinton depot on the right hand mainline track (left side as we face her in this picture.) It is headed by one of the beautiful Pacific's (4-6-2) number 474 that has taken her over the New River Subdivision. Waiting on the center track is a big shiny Mountain (4-8-2) number 540 ready to take the FFV over the Alleghany Subdivision.

This is a choice spot for photographers to catch both engines head-to-head. (Paul Dolkos)

The crew of our Pacific has gone off duty, checking in at the depot. A yard hostler has boarded the Pacific, which has been uncoupled from its train, pulled forward~ and is backing across the crossover from the middle siding track. The Mountain is still holding on the center track. The Pacific will back past its train, crossover the westbound main, and continue backing into the Hinton yards to be checked and serviced. (Paul Dolkos)

The big Mountain has now backed up and crossed over to the right hand eastbound main. Passengers and baggage have gotten on and off. With two short whistles the FFV is ready to depart Hinton. It is now 7 pm, nine minutes since it arrived! (Paul Dolkos)

It's 8:10 pm on a bright summer evening in 1938. The westbound Sportsman (number 47) has just arrived off of the Alleghany Subdivision at the Hinton station. There is a big Mountain engine, 4-8-2 in charge.

The engine crew leaves the engine here in front of the station and checks in at the station. They will probably retire to the YMCA on the hill behind the depot. (Paul Dolkos)

The Mountain engine (to the right) has been uncoupled from its train. A yard hostler has boarded the engine and is bringing it forward past the waiting Pacific (left) to continue into the yards. (Paul Dolkos)

The mainline crew has now backed the Pacific (number 494) in front of the station and has coupled up to the train. In the meantime, passengers and baggage have gotten on and off. (Bernard Kempinski)

With two short blasts of the whistle the Sportsman is ready to leave Hinton. It is now 8:18 pm, eight minutes since its arrival! (Paul Dolkos)

In the meantime still another coal drag has departed the Avis yard east of Hinton, heading up the Alleghany Subdivision to Alleghany, 50 miles to the east. Here is pusher H-7 (4-8-8-4). No 1540 with caboose behind passing MX Cabin. (Bernard Kempinski)

After the departure of the Sportsman, we climbed the steps to the YMCA, for a late bite to eat. This is a great place to talk railroading. After supper we stepped back to the yards to see a beautiful sunset. (Rob Downey)

A few minutes later we caught a Pacific (4-6-2) backing to the station to take charge of a westbound passenger train. (Rob Downey)

Chapter VI

ALDERSON - A GREAT PLACE TO SPEND TIME

As we leave Hinton eastbound, on the way to Alderson, we are on the Alleghany Subdivision. The grade up to the gap at Alleghany has already begun. We pass through the yards at Avis and MX Cabin, which is the eastern entry into the yards at Avis and Hinton. Our tracks now leave the banks of the New River. In about six miles we enter Little Bend Tunnel and then pop right into Big Bend Tunnel. In ten more miles we arrive at Alderson.

Alderson, originally known as Alderson's Ferry, was transformed in 1872 from a small unimportant river crossing into a thriving community with the arrival of the C & O Railway. Alderson grew to become an important station. As both freight and passenger business continued to increase, a new passenger depot was built in 1896. This was a standard C & O station design, erected at probably 200 locations. It had two waiting rooms on either side of the central ticket office, with its bay windows. An express and baggage room was located on the east end of the building.

In 1917 a 20-foot addition was added to the east end, with a second freight door to accommodate increased express shipments.

A GREAT PLACE TO SPEND TIME

Alderson is the home of the first federal, minimum-security prison for women. It was opened in 1927 through the encouragement of Eleanor Roosevelt, the future First Lady and Mabel Walker Willebrandt, the Assistant U.S. Attorney General. The prison has set a new and successful atmosphere for rehabilitation. The prison has a population of around 1,050. It is located on 105 acres of rolling hills. There are no fences or walls surrounding the prison. The inmates have been convicted of non-violent or white-collar crime. They sleep in bunk beds in dormitories and take care of their own needs, such as washing and ironing of clothes and bed covers. They have mandatory work schedules. During free time they may play volleyball, softball or tennis. The prison is nicknamed "Camp Cupcake."*

Today (summer of 1938), three westbound, and three eastbound passenger trains stop at Alderson every day: the FFV, the Sportsman, a local passenger train (number 13 westward and number 16 eastward.)

Continuing our climb east from Alderson towards Alleghany, we enter Mann's Tunnel, followed by Second Creek Tunnel. After passing Ronceverte we enter the short White Sulphur Tunnel, which brings us directly to White Sulphur Springs.

*After World War II, "Axis Sally" and "Tokyo Rose" spent time at Alderson Prison. Most recently, Martha Stewart spent five months here between 2004 and 2005.

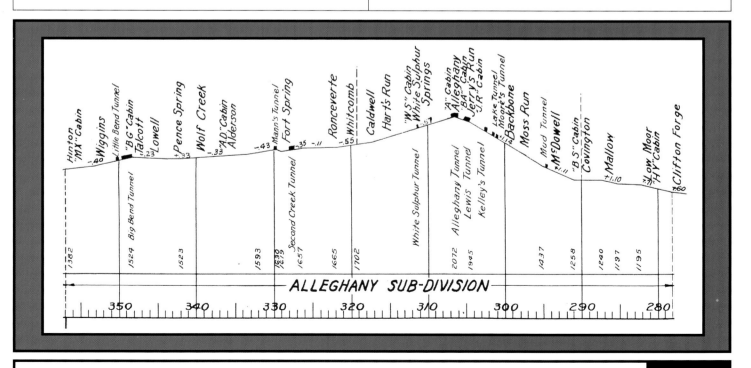

Classic Alderson Station in 1938. Eastbound train approaching. (Bernard Kempinski)

Alderson Station. Westbound train approaches. (Bernard Kempinski)

Actual Alderson Station in 1935

Chapter VII

WHITE SULPHUR SPRNGS - "NO SMOKE"

The spectacular Greenbrier Hotel is owned by the Chesapeake and Ohio Railway. In 1930 two new wings were added to the hotel. The Greenbrier had now reached its zenith, to match the style of its privileged guests as a national attraction.

For the convenience and safety of the preferred Greenbrier passengers, all trains stopped on the track next to the station platform. This necessitated the east-bound trains to cross over to the westbound main at the station.

Also, it was a rule of the C & O that there be no smoke from the engines as they passed the White Sulphur Springs station. From time to time an inspector would be at the station to observe this "no smoke" rule. Any engineer violating it would be noted and discipline would follow.

This is the only station on the entire C & O Railway with these two special dictates.

To coincide with the addition to the Greenbrier, a new White Sulphur Springs railway station was built in 1931. The new station is brick, painted white in the classic Georgian architectural style. It is located just across US Route 60 from the Greenbrier Hotel. Along with the new station, the tracks to accommodate the passenger cars were carefully laid out so that no switching of mainline trains was needed to drop off and pick up cars. A mainline passenger train crew would

have to be paid extra compensation if they had to do any switching of cars. Of course, the railway wanted to avoid this as well as the irritation to passengers of their cars being switched about. To accomplish this there are three sets of tracks: the pocket track, the house track and the park track. The pocket track is at the east end of the station; the house track runs around behind the station. The park track switches off the house track behind the station. (See the White Sulphur Springs Track Plan of ca. 1935 by Jessie Smith and Kevin Holland.) These station tracks have a capacity to park a total of 31 passenger cars. This is a big passenger car yard! Facilities had to be available for each car to plug in air conditioning as well as steam heat. All of this track capacity would be used from time to time for these private cars at special meets and conventions.

Train schedules were arranged so that passengers coming from both east and west arrived at White Sulphur Springs in the early morning so that they had a first full day at the great resort. The FFV left New York City in the evening and the Sportsman also left Detroit and Cincinnati in the evening. Both schedules gave their passengers a full night's sleep before their early morning arrival at the Greenbrier. Each train was met by the Greenbrier limousines for the convenient luxurious drive from the station to the hotel.

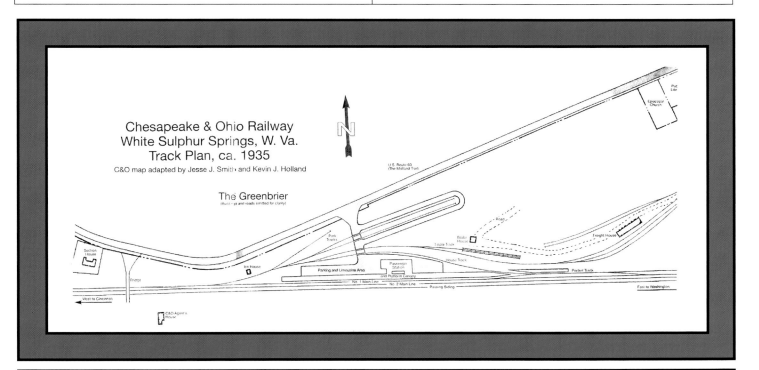

Chesapeake & Ohio Railway
White Sulphur Springs, W. Va.
Track Plan, ca. 1935
C&O map adapted by Jesse J. Smith and Kevin J. Holland

It is 12:10 AM. The George Washington has just arrived for a station stop. It is headed by one of the big new (1935) Greenbrier (4-8-4) engines. (Bernard Kempinski.)

We walk to the front of The George Washington for a picture of the big Greenbrier locomotive. There are very few people on the platform at this hour. (Bernard Kempinski)

It is 6:15 AM, at the first light of morning, the eastbound Sportsman, No. 4, is passing WS (White Sulphur) cabin. It will cross over to the westbound Mainline track (as do all passenger trains at White Sulphur), to be next to the station platform. (Bernard Kempinski)

The Sportsman arrives at White Sulphur Springs with passengers from Detroit Cleveland, Cincinnati and points west. ' These important trains, the FFV from the east and The Sportsman, arrive at White Sulphur in the early morning to give their premium passengers a full day at the Greenbrier Hotel. Here we get a good look at Mountain (4-8-2) number 540. (Bernard Kempinski)

Just five minutes later, at 6:20 AM, the FFV arrives White Sulphur Springs. The Pennsylvania Pullman from New York at the rear of the train is being dropped off on the "Pocket Track" at the east end of the station canopy. These important guests for the Greenbrier Hotel may continue resting in the cars until 8:00 AM. When the limousines from the hotel will pick them up. (Bernard Kempinski)

During No. 13's brief station stop, we step up to get a little closer view of the classic gleaming engine, number 543. (Bernard Kempinski).

It's 11:45 am. Local No. 13 has just arrived at White Sulphur Springs on time. Mountain type engine (4-8-2) is at the point. To the left is the "house track", running around behind the beautiful classic station. (Bernard Kempinski)

The George Washington at its midnight stop at White Sulphur Springs. (A posed publicity picture by the C & O)(C & O HS).

The same scene as modeled. (Rob Downey)

Westbound passenger train, stopped at White Sulphur Springs. (C & O HS)

The same scene as modeled. (Rob Downey)

Chapter VIII

ALLEGHANY - DANCE OF THE PUSHERS

Alleghany is an old Indian word, meaning "endless", to describe the entire eastern United States system of mountains. At the present time, the word Alleghany has been more restricted to describe a specific mountain range from north central Pennsylvania southwest into western Virginia.

The original spelling of Alleghany was with an "a". Later it was spelled with an "e" - Alleghany. The C & O elected to retain the original spelling with an "a."

From Hinton to Alleghany the railway grade keeps getting steeper, cumulating at 1.14%, at an altitude of 2072 feet. (The Alleghany station is 2 feet down grade at 2070 feet.)

In 1938 Alleghany is a remote and wonderful place, known by all too few people.

Coal drags from Hinton were headed by big articulated H-7s, 2-8-8-2s. These trains also all have a 2-8-8-2 pusher on the rear. There are 6 to 8 of these eastbound coal trains with their pushes every day and a corresponding number of empty coal trains returning west to the mines.

There are also three scheduled eastbound manifests and two scheduled westward manifests every day. In addition, there are local freight and passenger trains. Three crack passenger trains in each direction (The George Washington, FFV and the Sportsman) pass through every day. These will be headed by either a Mountain engine (4-8-2) or one of the big new (in 1935) Greenbrier's (4-8-4.) Passenger trains with over 12 heavyweight cars are double-headed, with these same engines. What a sight!

Each 24 hours about 36 trains pass through Alleghany. This is heavy mainline railroading!

"Simple Simon" articulated H-7 number 1572 on the point of an eastbound coal drag, emerges from the "old" Alleghany tunnel at Alleghany. Originally, this tunnel was double-tracked. Notice the wider tunnel openings. With the larger engines arriving, it was necessary to center the track in this tunnel and dig a second tunnel (to the right), completed in 1932. (Bernard Kempinski.)

The extra 1572 has pulled onto the eastbound siding at Alleghany and stopped. It has been assisted by pusher engine 1540 on the climb from Hinton. These wooden cabooses are always spotted behind the pusher. With the caboose in front of the pusher, all of that force could damage or collapse the caboose. The road locomotive on the head end has pulled the train away to stop at East Alleghany where it takes water and allows time for brakemen to set up the retainers on the hopper cars for the heavy down-grade operation into Covington. (Bernard Kempinski.)

Now, the pusher pulls back from the train. It will uncouple from the caboose on the siding and back around it over the double crossover on the main line (Bernard Kempinski).

The pusher, 1540, has run around the caboose, and is now preparing to push the caboose up to the end of the waiting coal train. (Bernard Kempinski)

The caboose is now coupled to the end of the train. (Bernard Kempinski)

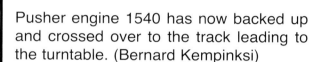

Pusher engine 1540 has now backed up and crossed over to the track leading to the turntable. (Bernard Kempinksi)

Our engine has entered the turntable. (Bernard Kempinski)

It is now being tuned for its trip light back to Hinton (Bernard Kempinski)

It has completed its 180 degree turn. (Bernard Kempinski)

It is now leaving the turntable, but is being held for the approach of a fast moving westbound manifest freight charging up the Alleghany grade. (Bernard Kempmski)

The manifest is headed by another H-7 articulated number 1556. Note the two entrances to the Lewis Tunnels in the background and the red signals protecting the movement. Whistle posts for the grade crossing at A Cabin are seen in the foreground also a dwarf signal for the crossovers. (Bernard Kempinski)

The manifest is now passing the Alleghany Station. Note the water tank on the hillside. (Bernard Kempinski)

It is now approaching the turnoff to the turntable. Maintenance sheds are in foreground. (Bernard Kempinski)

Engine Number 1556 is now roaring past A Cabin. (Bernard Kempinski)

After the passing of the manifest, our engine has now received clearance to enter the mainline. (Bernard Kempinski)

Our pusher engine passes A Cabin running light on its way back west to Hinton. Hinton is just 50 miles from Alleghany. The trip from Hinton takes about 4 to 5 hours; the turn around at Alleghany averages about an hour; the trip back to Hinton is about 2 hours. So you can see this represents about an 8-hour shift per crew. (Bernard Kempinski)

Alleghany 1935. (William Moneypenny-C & O HS)

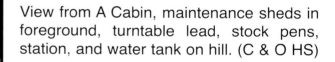

The model. (Rob Downey)

View from A Cabin, maintenance sheds in foreground, turntable lead, stock pens, station, and water tank on hill. (C & O HS)

The model. (Rob Downey)

The station at Alleghany. (C & O HS)

The model. (Rob Downey)

C&O engines K-3 #1245 and K-4 2762 in front of Alleghany Virginia station. #2762 is working as a pusher while #1245 heads up east bound freight on siding. Alleghany subdivision, Location code 23229. (Photo by B.F. Cutler.)

The model.
(Rob Downey)

The station at Alleghany is a busy place in 1938. (C&O HS)

Engine on the turntable at Alleghany. (C & O HS)

The model. (Rob Downey)

Chapter IX

THE 1938 ENGINES OF THE NEW RIVER AND ALLEGHANY SUBDIVISION

In 1938 the C & O Railway believed that each engine type was designed for a specific purpose; heavy freight or light freight, heavy passenger or light passenger, mainline or branchline. This resulted in a wonderful assortment of steam engines. The following classes of engines are depicted in this book.

NEW RIVER SUBDIVISION

Freight Engines		Where Used
0-8-0	Switch Engines Class C-I6	(1) Hinton Yards-one in east & one in west end; three shifts, 24 hours per day. (2) Quinnimont in the Wye
2-8-0	Consolidation Class G-9	(1) Thurmond-mine runs (2) Laurel Creek Branch
2-8-2	Mikado Class K-2 and K-3	(1) Mainline manifest freights (2) Mainline local freights
2-6-6-2	Mallet Class H-4	Thurmond-mine runs
2-8-8-2	Simple Articulated Class H-7	(1) Mainline coal trains (2) Mainline manifest freights

Passenger Engines		Where Used
4-6-2	Pacific Class F-I7 and F-I9	Mainline passenger trains

ALLEGHANY SUBDIVISION

Freight Engines		Where Used
2-8-2	Mikado Class K-2 and K-3	Mainline local freights
2-8-8-2	Simple Articulated Class H-7	(1) Mainline manifest freights (2) Mainline coal trains

Passenger Engines		Where Used
4-8-2	Mountain Class J-1 and J-2	Mainline passenger trains
4-8-4	Greenbrier Class J-3	Mainline passenger trains

0-8-0 Switch Engines, Class C-16 In 1938, Class C-16 Switch Engines are the C&O's most numerous and modern class. The first 65 of these engines we purchased in 1930. They could be found in virtually every yard of the C&O from east to west. They are numbered from 175 to 239. (Bernard Kempinski)

2-8-0 Consolidation, Class G-9 Fifty engines in this group were purchased in 1909 and basically followed previous designs, which had proved quite successful. They are numbered 1010 to 1059. They are used for smaller mine runs, mainline locals, and branch line passenger service. Engine 1028 is on the wye at Quinnimont preparing to take the local up the Laurel Creek Branch. (Bernard Kempinski)

2-8-2 Mikado, Class K-2 and K-3

As trains became longer and heavier, the Consolidations were double-headed even triple-headed. It became evident that a larger, more powerful engine was needed. . After several tests, the K-2 and K - 3 were born in 1924. Fifty K-2' s numbered 1160 to 1209 and fifty K-3's numbered 1210 to 1259 were received. The railway was so pleased with these that fifty more K-3's were ordered in 1925, numbered 2300 to 2349.

In the following years, the K-2's and K-3's were the mainstay of the C&O manifest freights on the low-gradient divisions and local freights on the entire railway. Here we see a K-3 dropping off some cars at the Alleghany station. (Bernard Kempinski)

2-6-6-2 Mallet, Class H-4

After successful tests, it was decided that this compound Mallet was the engine for hauling coal drags over the mountain regions. As a result, a total of 150 were ordered from 1912 to 1918; numbered 1325 to 1474. These engines were never used on the mainlines, but used exclusively on the branches to the coal mines. Here we see H-4, 1397 "at home" in the Thurmond yard, ready to serve the many branches out of Thurmond. By 1938, 74 engines of this class were retired! (Bernard Kempinski)

2-8-8-2 Simple Articulated, Class H-7

By the early 1920' s, Mallet type engines much larger than the C&O's 2-6-6-2 were in use by many railroads. The C&O had a problem. Due to the many tunnels on the Alleghany Subdivision with close clearances, the large front low-pressure cylinders would not clear. The solution was an engine with all four cylinders to be smaller high-pressure, single expansion. To produce this great volume of steam, the largest possible boiler and firebox was needed. This left insufficient room for the air pumps normally mounted on the sides of the boiler. To solve this problem the pumps were mounted, one on each side of the front of the smoke box beneath the overhanging Elesco feedwater heater. With the bell centered below the feedwater heater and the headlight positioned low on the pilot deck, the new C&O "look" was born. This look was to be continued for years to come on many C&O engines.

The first 25 2-8-8-2, H-7's were received in 1924 and numbered 1540 to 1564. Another order of 20 was received in 1926, numbered 1570 to 1589. Their official name was Chesapeakes, but this never caught on. The crews more popularly called them "Simple Simons."

So in 1938, there are 45 of these engines, working mostly on the Alleghany Subdivision mainlines between Hinton and Clifton Forge. The eastbound coal trains also used the H-7's as a pusher. This H-7, 1564, is on the turntable at Alleghany, ready to return to Hinton. (Bernard Kempinski)

4-8-2 Mountain, Class J-I and J-2

By 1910, established passenger train procedure on the Alleghany Subdivision called for one F-15 Pacific on trains up to six cars. Since traffic had increased to the point that many trains had ten or twelve cars, it was necessary to double-head the power. Of course, this was expensive.

After extensive studies, it was determined that to do the required job, an engine with eight drive wheels (rather than the six drivers of the Pacifics) was needed. The resulting engine, 4-8-2, was the largest and most powerful simple locomotive ever built. The resulting tests of these new locomotives far exceeded the expectations of both the railway and the builder. The initial class of three engines was classed J-l.

In the following years, steel passenger cars replaced the wooden cars. In 1918, 1919, and 1923 seven more Mountain type engines were purchased and classed J-2. They had higher boiler pressure and larger drivers. In 1930, these engines were overhauled with Worthington feedwater heaters and flying-pumps on the front end, emerging in the "George Washington" styling associated with the F-19 Pacifics. Here is J-2, 543, ready to leave the Hinton station on the eastward climb up the Alleghany Subdivision. (Bernard Kempinski)

4-6-2 Pacific, Class F-17 and F-19

The original five F-I7's were delivered in 1914 and believed to be the largest Pacifics built at that time. These five engines were extensively rebuilt in 1930, receiving Worthington feedwater heaters, Boxpok drivers, and Delta trailing trucks and the flying-pumps front-end styling. These rebuilt engines ruled the Cincinnati Division in 1938.

In 1926, the C&O received an additional five Pacifics, to become F-19, numbers 490 to 494. This was the most famous of the C&O Pacifics with the flying pumps, Elesco feedwater heater, and low-mounted headlight.

These were the engines used to introduce both The Sportsman in 1930 and The George Washington in 1932. These engines were always immaculately groomed. Here is a classic Pacific number 494 in front of the Hinton Station. (Bernard Kempinski)

4-8-4 Greenbrier, Class J-3

In the early 1930's, the C&O completely renovated its through passenger services with the introduction of The Sportsman between Detroit and Newport News in 1930 and The George Washington between Cincinnati and Washington in 1932. The "FFV" was also re-equipped and modernized at this time, resulting in three heavy, deluxe, air-conditioned trains on tight, demanding schedules. Passenger service was the road's prestige and anything less than the best was unthinkable.

In order to keep pace with these demands, new power was required. It was decided that a 4-8-4 wheel arrangement would produce the desired product.

In 1935, five big new 4-8-4 engines were received and immediately began attacking the Alleghany Subdivision with a vengeance. They performed superbly. Fourteen heavyweight cars were the standard for a J-3. These first five J-3's had the headlight in the center of the smoke box, (later orders had the low-mounted headlight), these first five were changed to comply with the C&O look.

The late 1930's were indeed the days of wine and roses for C&O passenger service, and both are on the tables of the diners. Here is J-3, 603 on the center pocket track at the Hinton Station. When its charge arrives, it will switch over to the eastbound main in front of the camera to couple up to its train. (Bernard Kempinski)

Chapter X

THE FFV, THE SPORTSMAN, AND THE GEORGE WASHINGTON

By 1889 the initial construction of the Chesapeake and Ohio was completed. It was time to gain recognition of the completed railway. How better to achieve this than the introduction of a brand new luxury train? The train was to be the FAST FLYING VIRGINIAN (FFV.) It would be one of America's premier trains in the 1890's. The new cars would have vestibules, quite new at the time, which allowed passengers to pass safely from car to car while the train was in motion. The new cars were to have electric lights, replacing cheaper gas lights, and steam heating, replacing dangerous stoves and ceiling fans for comfort in the summer. While most passenger cars were painted dark green, the C & O painted its new cars bright orange or yellow, with a maroon letter board and red wheels.

The importance of vestibules cannot be overstated. The initial advertising of the FFV was called the "Vestibule Limited," and the full name became "The Fast Flying Virginian Vestibule Limited."

The FFV was an immediate success. In the first year, passenger revenues were up 75%, while the number of passengers carried increased 90%! Over the years the cars of the successful FFV were continually upgraded, and by 1913 the wood cars were replaced by all-steel cars.

In 1924 the C & O discontinued the orange/yellow color of its passenger cars in favor of an olive green.

The great Virginia resorts, Hot Springs and White Sulphur Springs, had always been major destinations for C & O passengers. With the C & O purchase of the Greenbrier Hotel in 1910, major advertising was now directed to this resort. The FFV was scheduled with perfect departure time from both New York and Cincinnati to give early morning arrival at White Sulphur Springs.

The FFV was always the grande dame of the C & O passenger fleet. It was the longest-running and largest revenue-producing train, exceeding its later sisters, The Sportsman and The George Washington.

In the summer of 1938 there is one Pennsylvania Pullman from New York that arrives at 6:20 am on the westbound FFV, (number 3) at White Sulphur Springs every day, seven days a week. It could be accompanied by additional cars from the east and C & O Pullmans from Washington, but these additional cars were not arriving every day.

There is some uncertainty as to which track this car or cars were "dropped off' on. According to Mr. Roy Long,

THE "Vestibule Limited"

F. F. V.

FACILITIES such as Springs-goers have never before enjoyed will be offered this season by the inauguration of the Vestibule Limited, which runs from Cincinnati to Washington and New York without change, with Vestibule Sleeper from Louisville to New York, reaching White Sulphur for breakfast and other mountain resorts in the early morning.

The Limited will consist of Combined Car, Palace Day Coach with Smoking Saloon, Dining Car and Sleeping Cars, vestibuled from end to end — heated by steam drawn from the engine and lighted by electricity. Dining cars will run through from Cincinnati to New York without change, enabling passengers to dine leisurely without the apprehension that their meals will be unpleasantly terminated by the side-tracking of the car.

The cuisine will be under the immediate direction of the Pullman Company; meals will be served *table d'hote* at uniform rate of $1.00. The vestibule features commend themselves readily to every traveler; the vibration of the train is reduced to a minimum by the absence of sharp points of contact between the cars, the passage from one car to another can be made as freely and safely as in a private residence, while the crystal enclosures forming the vestibule greatly adds to the beauty of the train.

telegraph operator at White Sulphur Springs, this car was left on the pocket track. (See track diagram, Chapter VII.)

However, the eastbound Sportsman (No.4) is scheduled to arrive five minutes earlier at 6:15am from Detroit and other points west. It will cross over to the westbound mainline track to be next to the platform canopy, so that guests will not have to cross any tracks. The Sportsman does not often have cars to set out, but if it did, it would have to run around the house track and leave its car(s) there. As Jessie Smith points out, in his excellent article on White Sulphur Springs in the C & O History Magazine of July/August 2003, any cars on the pocket track will block the eastern access to the house track. Realizing the problem, it seems logical, on the rare times that The Sportsman has a car or cars to drop of the FFV would place its car(s) on the house track to leave the pocket track free for the Sportsman's car(s).

The following pictures will explain the entire sequence of this interesting Pennsylvania Pullman on its daily trip from New York to White Sulphur Springs and return.

No. 3 gets an inspection as she pauses in the early morning at Hinton, W. Va in the mid-1930's. (C & O HS Collection)

Interior of FFV diner #452 at the Pullman shops in 1889. Note electric fixtures over the tables and oil fixtures in the clerestory. Imagine how ornately cluttered this scene would have been with the tables fully set. (Photo from Smithsonian Institution)

Interior view of C&O Pullman Alderson as built in 1907. (Photo from Smithsonian Institution)

Vestibules were introduced into American passenger railroading in 1887. and immediately gained widespread popularity. Most important name trains were equipped with them by the late 1890's. The FFV was among the first all-vestibuled limiteds in operation. This Pullman Company photo shows the ornate ironwork around the narrow vestibule from an FFV car of 1889. (Photo from the Smithsonian Institution Collection)

Although wide-vestibules were standard in 1899, this narrow-vestibule combine was built for FFV service in 1899 to replace an earlier car lost in a wreck. (Photo from Smithsonian Institution Collection)

One of the few surviving photos of original 1889 FFV equipment is this fine Pullman builder's view of diner #452. A classic car for a classic train at the forefront of technology in its day. (Photo from Smithsonian Institution collection)

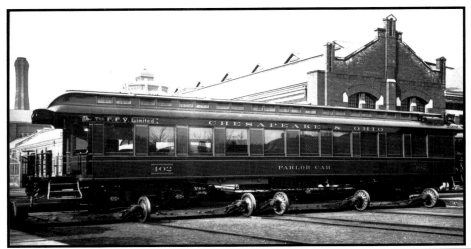

This parlor/buffet car was built for FFV service in 1894 and ran on the daylight portions of the trip between Hinton and Cincinnati for many years. (Photo courtesy of Charles Clegg)

Pullman 12/1 sleeper Alderson was built as part of the FFV upgrade equipment in 1907. (Photo from Smithsonian Institution)

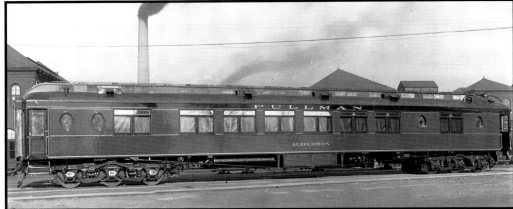

The FFV (#3) arrives at White Sulphur Springs station at 6:20 am. The last car, a Pullman, of the Pennsylvania from New York City is dropped on the White Sulphur station pocket track. The passengers on this car will not be disturbed in their sleep. They have until 8:00 in the morning to get up to meet the limousine and depart for the Greenbrier Hotel, just across the street. (Bernard Kempinski)

Later this morning at 11:45 am westbound train #13 picks up the Pennsylvania Pullman from the pocket track at White Sulphur and takes it to Hinton. (Paul Dolkos)

Westbound train 13 arrives at Hinton at 1:30 pm. (Paul Dolkos)

Train #13 is headed by Mountain #543 (4-8-2) as it arrives off the Alleghany Subdivision. (Bernard Kempinski)

In preparation to heading down river on the New River Subdivision, the Mountain engine is uncoupled from the train, as seen on the right. It will now pull forward, switch off the mainline, and proceed into the Hinton yards. Waiting to take over for the New River Subdivision is the beautiful Pacific (4-6-2) on the left. (Paul Dolkos)

Pacific 494 coupled to train #13 and <u>almost</u> ready to depart. (Paul Dolkos)

The train pulls forward past the station and stops. (Paul Dolkos)

A switch engine (0-8-0) has come up behind the train to take off the Pennsylvania Pullman. Train 13 proceeds on down the New River Subdivision. (Paul Dolkos)

Here we see the switch engine pushing the Pennsylvania Pullman into the Hinton Yards. It will be serviced and cleaned in preparation for its departure for New York later this evening. (Paul Dolkos)

It is now 6:51 pm, and train number 6 (the eastbound FFV) is just arriving at the Hinton station right on time. As it comes off the New River Subdivision it is powered by one of the C & O's Pacific's (4-6-2.) It is still on the east-bound mainline, to the left in the photo. (This picture represents the great photo opportunity at Hinton.) The big Mountain engine (4-8-2) is parked on the middle track ready to take over. (Paul Dolkos)

The Pacific is uncoupled from its train and pulled forward to switch over the pocket track. The Mountain is still resting in its location, visible in front of the Pacific. (Paul Dolkos)

The Pacific has now backed across the mainline and backed into the Hinton yards for servicing. The Mountain has backed from the center track to the crossover track and pulled forward to the eastbound mainline track and then backed down on the waiting train. ~ The train is uncoupled in the middle behind the last coach, and the engineer pulls the front part of the train a car length past the crossover track. Switch engine 175 pushes the Pennsylvania Pullman through the crossover to be coupled behind the last coach. (Paul Dolkos)

The switch engine is uncoupled from the PRR Pullman and returns to the Hinton Yards. (Bernard Kempinski)

The crossover switch is aligned with the eastbound main and the engineer backs the train to couple the PRR Pullman to the rest of the train. The Pennsylvania Pullman is now in its proper place in the FFV, ready to go to White Sulphur Springs and pick up the passengers returning to New York tonight. On the trip from New York to White Sulphur this special Pennsylvania Pullman, and any other cars for White Sulphur, could be put on the end of the train behind the Salon because this entire trip was at night, so no one would be looking out the rear of the Salon car. On the return trip to New York part of trip is in daylight, and the passengers need access to the diner. (Bernard Kempinski)

THE SPORTSMAN

The late 1930's were probably the greatest days for the C & O's passenger fleet. The equipment was the best and latest, service was honed to perfection, and the roadbed arguably the best maintained in the country. The railway was in a strong financial position due to the coal business. The C & O liked its passenger trains and lavished attention on them far exceeding their revenue value.

The introduction of The Sportsman on March 30, 1930 was a spectacular affair. The train was viewed by 103,816 on its eleven-day public exhibition tour before being put into regular service between Detroit and Old Point Comfort, Virginia.

The Sportsman provided the first direct service between the financial and manufacturing centers of the Mid-West and Great Lakes with Virginia and the eastern seaboard.

There are Pullmans with drawing rooms, compartments, sections and berths. The new salon cars with a seating capacity of only 45 provided comfort and spaciousness. The seats are arranged in pairs on one side of the aisle and singly on the other. These chairs can be turned and swiveled to make a grouping of four as well as parties of two. This is all available at no extra fare. While The FFV and The George Washington are night trains, The Sportsman passes through some of the most beautiful and historic areas in the country in daylight hours.

As a personal note, at the age of 10, in 1936, I was taken by my parents on my first trip. It was on The Sportsman from Cincinnati to Old "Point Comfort, Virginia. We left the Cincinnati Union Terminal at about 10:00 pm. My parents allowed me to share the lower berth of the Pullman next to the window with my mother. What a thrill, to look out the window into the night as we left Cincinnati to cross the Ohio River, to see the lights of Covington and Newport, to see the flashing red lights of the grade crossings and hear their bells. Before long this all faded away, we were in the dark countryside, and I fell asleep.

With the daylight of the next morning, my parents explained that the C & O allowed us to move into the Salon car at the rear of the train without paying an extra Pullman fare for this part of the trip. (Even better, the Salon car was more comfortable than the Pullman day seats.) I immediately took up position looking out the rear window of the car with my Kodak box camera. Believe it or not, many of those pictures from a moving train turned out O.K.

Upon reaching Old Point Comfort we were met by a driver and taken to see the remains of the first permanent English Settlement at Jamestown, the battlefield at Yorktown and the disappearing coastal defense guns. From there we went to Washington and continued our trip. For me, the highlight was the ride on The Sportsman.

It's a summer evening in 1938.

Passengers are entering the beautiful new (just completed in 1933) Art Deco Cincinnati Union Terminal. They are passing through the huge entry rotunda to the concourse and on to track 14.

6:01pm

This is the moment!

The pride of the C & O's passenger fleet, The George Washington, leaves Cincinnati, Ohio, for Washington, D.C.

It's the same summer evening in Washington, D.C.

Passengers are entering the front doors of Washington Union Station. They are passing through the magnificent Main hall to the Station Concourse and to the boarding gate.

6:01pm

This is the moment!

The pride of the C & O's passenger fleet, The George Washington leaves Washington for Cincinnati.

Our train eastbound from Cincinnati is under the charge of a gleaming, high-stepping Pacific (4-6-2) engine. It has already crossed the Ohio River, passed through Covington and Newport, Kentucky and is now charging up the "Race Track" division along the Ohio River. Our passengers have checked their berths and bedrooms and have plenty of time to enjoy the scenery along the Ohio River while it is still light. In good time they will stroll to the dining car, Gatsby's Tavern. There is just nothing like "dinner in the diner." Just look at your 75-cent dinner!

After dinner, passengers may return to their bedroom or to the Solarium (Observation) car, Commander-in-Chief at the rear of the train, for a drink, to read the newspaper, for good conversation, or to listen to the radio as darkness descends. The George Washington was designed for the business person's travel between Cincinnati and Washington. Imagine the convenience of boarding this train after a full days' work in either city, having a full nights sleep and arriving early the next morning, refreshed for a full day in the other city.

George Washington, "first in war, first in peace and first in the hearts of our countrymen" can well be considered the father of the Chesapeake and Ohio Railway.

On April 24, 1932, at the height of the great depression, the C & O introduced the best of its great new premier trains. It was fitting that it would be named The George Washington. The new heavy weight passenger cars were all air-conditioned. The first fully air-conditioned train in America!

Wasn't this a poor time to invest in a new passenger train? Most railroads were feeling hard-times of the depression, but not the C & O. Their main, and very profitable business, was hauling coal, and coal was king in commercial industry as well as retail home heating. The C & O was in a strong cash position. What better way to reach the public than with a beautiful, new state-of-the-art train? Furthermore, the travel between Cincinnati and Washington was increasing, even though there was plenty of competition.

In 1938 Cincinnati had 452,852 people and was the 17th largest city in the country. Washington had a population of 663,153 and was the 11th largest city. However, between these two rather secondary cities, there were five railroads offering daily multiple passenger service. They were the Chesapeake & Ohio, the Norfolk and Western, the Baltimore and Ohio, the New York Central and the Pennsylvania railroads.

Through the course of the evening, we have made a few stops at Ashland, Kentucky, Huntington, Charleston and Handley, West Virginia. One by one the passengers have left the Solarium car and returned to their berths or rooms. For the past hour-and-a-half, The George Washington has been gliding smoothly along the New River on the New River Subdivision.

It is now 12:43 as our train flashes past CW Cabin, exactly two miles west of the Hinton station, but she is already slowing down for the station stop. The countryside is pitch black, but the lights on the top floor of CW Cabin are bright, for CW Cabin never closes. As the George Washington rounds the bend with the New River on the right and the dark hillside on the left, the Hinton yards come into view. What a contrast-there are lights everywhere; the powerful floodlights atop the giant coaling tower face both east and west. The smoke and steam rising from the many engines in the yards is illuminated like white clouds by the giant floodlights. There are hundreds of lights all along the servicing track at the small grand central building, at the inspection pits, at the water columns, on all sides and under the great coaling tower, at the three cinder conveyors, at the engine washing platforms, at the turntable, roundhouse, shops, the Mallet engine house, the icing house and platform, and the many small shanties to our right along the river.

Hinton is indeed a beehive of activity day and night. However, very few lights show through the windows of our train, most everyone is asleep as we glide smoothly and quietly without the slightest bump to a stop in front of the Hinton station. It is now 12:46 am, we are right on time. In the station, the dispatcher's office at the bay window is brightly lit, lights show through the window of the passenger waiting rooms, and the baggage room on the first floor, but the offices on the second and third floors are dark. Very few passengers on the train will be aware of what is happening, for this is the way it should be. The crews are very much aware of not disturbing the sleep of these passengers. As we pulled up in front of the Hinton station on the eastbound track, there is already one of the big new (in 1935) Greenbrier, Class J 4-8-4 engines facing east on the center track between the east and west mainline tracks.

Just as soon as our engine stopped, a switchman is already standing by at this point to uncouple our Pacific 4-6-2. It now pulls forward a few engine lengths until the front of the Pacific is opposite the front of the waiting Greenbrier. (These are the great daytime pictures we see of the engine changes in front of the Hinton Depot.) The switch is thrown behind the Pacific, the headlight goes dim, and the tender light is on as it quietly backs up light across the crossover of the westbound main and into the entrance of the yard.

For a moment, let's look back at the station. The switch behind the big Greenbrier on the center track has been thrown, it is backing a short distance to clear the switch to the crossover to the eastbound main. The switch is then thrown, it moves quietly and slowly forward to come upon the eastbound main in front of our waiting train. Again, the eastern switch is thrown and our Greenbrier backs down slowly on the waiting train, just touching the couplers. The airlines are connected and checked. Nine minutes have passed. In addition to the crew changes, a few passengers have gotten on and off and baggage has been loaded and unloaded. The engine headlight goes bright, two quick whistles, and the George Washington easily and quietly pulls out of Hinton at 12:55am, "right on the advertised." Again we are surrounded by about total darkness as the city lights quickly fade away. We are gaining speed rapidly, and just get a quick look at the lighted second floor of MX Cabin at the eastern approach to the Avis and Hinton yards; again it never closes.

Hinton is near the western base of the Alleghany mountains. For this reason, it is necessary to change from the smaller Pacific (4-6-2) engine to the large Greenbrier (4-8-4) for the climb over the mountains. We are now on the Alleghany Subdivision and have started up the grade to the pass at Alleghany.

After crossing the mountains at Alleghany, we will descend to Clifton Forge, Virginia at this point the Greenbrier engine will be replaced by another smaller Pacific engine for the more level trip into Washington.

When our passengers awake in the morning in Washington, most will be unaware of all of this. And this is as it should be.

CINCINNATI UNION TERMINAL

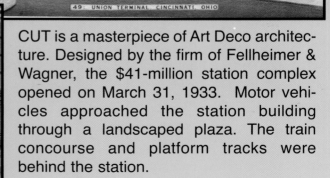

49. UNION TERMINAL CINCINNATI, OHIO

CUT is a masterpiece of Art Deco architecture. Designed by the firm of Fellheimer & Wagner, the $41-million station complex opened on March 31, 1933. Motor vehicles approached the station building through a landscaped plaza. The train concourse and platform tracks were behind the station.

It's track 14 in the concourse of the Cincinnati Union Terminal. The George Washington is almost ready to depart for Washington at 6:01 pm. (C & O HS)

The magnificent waiting room, with mahogany benches, of the Washington Union Station. (Postcard from the collection of Thomas W. Dixon, Jr.)

Washington Union Station is called the most civilized transportation center in America. (Postcard)

C & O diner 965, Gadsby's Tavern as it is on The George Washington. (Photo by K.L. Miller)

Passengers at Washington Union Station preparing to board *The George Washington* for Cincinnati. (C&O HS)

Dining on *The George Washington*, a C & O ad. (C & O HS)

It is 12:43 am, as The George Washington approaches CW Cabin, the western entrance to the Hinton yards, with a shiny Pacific (4-6-2) on the head end. (Paul Dolkos)

The solarium car, Commander-in-Chief, is just passing CW Cabin. (Bernard Kempinski)

From the westbound mainline track, We catch another view of the solarium car of The George Washington. (Paul Dolkos)

The George Washington has passed CW Cabin and is rounding the bend In the New River with the Hinton yards on the left. (Bernard Kempinski)

"The George" has stopped at the Hinton Station. The mainline crew has left the train to check in at the station, and if they live out of town, will retire to the YMCA on the hill behind the station. (Paul Dolkos)

This rarely seen picture of The George Washington, headed by the Pacific, nose-to-nose with the big Greenbrier (4-8-4), on the center track to take the train out of Hinton onto the Alleghany Subdivision. As you will note, there is not much activity on the station platform at this hour. (Paul Dolkos)

A yard hostler has boarded the Pacific as it is uncoupled from the train. He has pulled forward to the switch and is now backing over the crossover to the center track. He will proceed across to the westbound mainline and into the Hinton yards for servicing. (Paul Dolkos)

The Pacific has moved into the yards. The new mainline Crew is on board the Greenbrier, and is backing to the crossover to swing over to the eastbound mainline track. Note that some lights have come on in the YMCA, as the crew arrives up there. (Paul Dolkos)

The Greenbrier is now coupled to The George Washington and ready to depart. We arrived at 12:46 (right on time.) It is now 12:55, we have been here 9 minutes! (Paul Dolkos)

Again we see the Greenbrier backing to the crossover to put it on the Eastbound main and to couple onto the train. Note that all the houses and buildings on Front Street in Hinton are dark. The station will be open all night as there are many more passenger trains due. (Paul Dolkos)

With two short whistles, the George Washington smoothly and quietly departs the depot at Hinton. (Paul Dolkos)

Our eastbound George Washington is only five minutes out of Hinton when it meets the westbound George at 1:00 AM with Mountain engine number 540 on the point. (Bernard Kempinski)

On another night, we found Mountain 540 returning from Hinton and meeting the westbound George Washington. (Bernard Kempinski)

Chapter XI

ABOUT THE C&O MODEL RAILWAY

The following ten ideas are thoughts you might like to consider if you are planning a model railroad.

1. Cove the corners

The room corners between side walls, and the walls and ceiling limit the railroad to a room. By coving the corners, you eliminate the confines of a room and expand the scene.

This is so fast, easy, and inexpensive compared to the time and money spent on the layout, it is a shame not to do it. It should be done first, before the layout is started.

I use 1/8 inch thick Masonite, bent into the corners between the walls and ceiling. Draw a line on the ceiling and the wall, put in a drywall screw, left out about an inch on both ends of your line. Simply press the Masonite into the corner, the drywall screws will hold it. Gently screw in the screws with the head up against the Masonite.

There are two things to do before putting up the Masonite. (1) Roll on a coat of polyurethane on both sides. This keeps moisture out of the Masonite so that it will not expand and contract and crack between the different joints. (2) If you would like to have stars on your ceiling at night, now is the time to tack two or three courses of those cheap clear white Christmas tree strands around the top of the wall near the ceiling. When your Masonite cove is in place, simply drill random holes about 1/8 inch in size, voila, instant stars! Do not worry about replacing burned out bulbs; they are not on that long. After the cove is in place between the walls and ceiling, we need a cove in the comers.

Easy. Just cut a Gothic arch on the short side of a piece of Masonite. There is no magic formula, just cut a Gothic arch that looks good to you. I have done this on three layouts, and every arch works. You will press this piece of Masonite into the corner, overlapping some of the cove in place between the walls and ceiling. The Gothic arch will be at the top, well out on the ceiling. This arch compensates the bend in the corner. It will be held in place by drywall screws in the side coves and ceiling.

Now is the time to discover that you, too, can be a drywall expert. We need to tape and fill the joints around the Masonite. At your local hardware or home center, pick up a roll of drywall tape, a bucket of drywall compound, and two putty knives - one about 2 inches wide and one 3 1/2 to 4 inches wide.

With your 2-inch knife, spread a thin layer of compound on the joint. Tear off a strip of tape and press it into the compound. With your wider knife, spread another thin cover of compound over the tape. Keep both of these compound applications fairly thin. If you get it too thick, it will crack when it dries. After a couple of days come back with another thin coat of compound over the first. It may require a third coat; this is okay. After the last coat of compound is dry, sand over it with some medium-fine sandpaper to get a smooth joint. There you have it!

In an effort to make the comer coving visible, we turned the lighting for this photo at an unnatural angle. You can see the corner and the Gothic arch cut at the top. (Bernard Kempinski)

Here is the same comer (over Quinnimont) with the natural room light. (Bernard Kempinski)

2. Lighting

Most model railroaders construct valances over the scenes with lights behind, to illuminate the scenery. I have another thought. On three layouts, I have used ordinary recessed hi-hat fixtures with 65-watt flood bulbs in the ceiling over the aisles. These are spaced about two feet apart. This results in even light on the scenery on both sides of the aisle with no shadows.

Should you decide that you want to operate your layout at night, these ceiling lights can be set to dim automatically and adjusted by means of a fast clock. Also, a sunset and sunrise can be incorporated. The electronics to accomplish this and more are available from Rail-Lynx.*

The sunrise and sunset really gets the oohs and aahs from the visitors. To do this, attach a 1" x 2" riser up from the benchwork against the wall about 16 inches apart and cut about 8 inches below the top of your scenery. Another 1" x 2" will rest horizontally on top of these risers. This will be wrapped with those inexpensive Christmas tree bulbs in red and/or orange. This will cast a beautiful glow up on your walls and coving at the interval between day and night. (See pictures of Hinton yards).

At night, you will have stars in the sky and lights in the buildings. (Rail-Lynx can also program the building lights to come on at different times).

*Rail-Lynx, 327 West Johnston Street. Allentown, PA 18103, (610) 351~0672

This picture shows some of the recessed ceiling lights over the aisle. The invisible room corner is to the right in the picture. The wall above the horizon is coved to the ceiling. The lights not on are for nighttime lighting. (Rob Downey)

Here is a sequence to watch the sunset. The center of the sunset is over the Hinton yards. (Bernard Kempinski)

This scene is just to the west of Hinton. (Bernard Kempinski)

The same location as the sunset is almost complete. (Bernard Kempinski)

Here we see a brilliant sunrise over Quinnimont. (Rob Downey)

3. Painting

My train room is 21 feet by 31 feet. I started with a five-gallon can of medium flat sky blue and three-gallon cans of flat white paint. Of course, the amount of paint needed will depend on the size of your room. Remember, you only need this paint to go a little below the top of your background scenery, not to the floor. Start rolling on your blue paint in the middle of the ceiling and work out evenly on all sides from the middle. As your five-gallon can goes down about every two inches, add about one inch of white. Keep working evenly on all sides and you will notice that the sky will get gradually lighter. Continue this procedure right down from the top of the walls to a little lower than the top of your scenery. Remember, your scenery is about two inches away from the walls-the space for the horizon sunset and sunrise Christmas lights. As in nature, the sky is less blue as you approach the horizon.

This view shows the recessed ceiling lights over an aisle, the coving between ceiling and wall and the sky becoming lighter toward the horizon. (No photo floods were used). (Bernard Kempinski)

4. Horizon

Remember, most railroads follow streams and rivers; they are in low places. Even going through mountains, they follow the lowest pass. In viewing your layout, you will not have long vistas and views if you want the railroad to be at or near eye level. An important rule to remember is that your horizon should be at or above the eye level of the viewer. Only if you are in an airplane will you be above the horizon. So in most cases you will not have to worry about painting those far distant mountains.

View of horizon. It is above eye level; the railway is following the New River through a valley. (Rob Downey)

5. Clouds

Several people have remarked how great my clouds look. This is ironic because they represent almost zero time and effort. Take a few pieces of light or medium cardboard, cut out one long side with some puffs and billows that look like the tops of clouds upside down. With this side on the bottom of the cardboard, hold it against the wall and spray on flat white paint up to your cardboard. Let your white paint taper off to the base of the cloud. Repeat this with a few other pieces of cardboard so they will not all look the same. There you have it - instant clouds.

Here are some white billowy clouds floating over the Hinton yards on a sunny afternoon. (Bernard Kempinski)

6. Track Plan

There are unlimited choices of track plans, whether you are following a prototype railroad or creating a pike of your own choosing. There are scores of excellent books on the subject of developing a track plan.

My layout is in a 21 x 31 foot room. It represents about 100 miles of the C & O between Hawks Nest to the west and the twin Lewis tunnels to the east of Alleghany at the West Virginia state line. Hinton is the focal point. To the west of Hinton is the New River Subdivision on the lower level of the layout. To the east of Hinton is the Alleghany Subdivision on the upper level. The two levels are accomplished without a shelf for the upper level, rather using the natural hillside to separate the two levels. I was careful not to have a scene or point of interest on one level directly above or below a scene on the other level.

Looking at the layout at any point from the aisles, east is always to the viewer's right and left is to the west, just as on a map. Since the model railroad is designed for walk around control, the engineer running a train has the feeling of really going from east to west or vice versa. The grades on both Subdivisions are an approximation of the prototype. From Hawks Nest along the New River Subdivision there is a slight increase in elevation all the way to Hinton. On the Alleghany Subdivision, the railway climbs a steeper grade from Hinton east to Alleghany, then descends again, continuing eastward into the staging area under Hinton. Here it is connected to the track coming out of staging at Hawks Nest.

This enables the loaded coal trains to keep moving from west to east and the empty coal trains to keep returning from east to west. The fly-over tracks at both ends allow passenger trains to return from their Subdivision with the same engine and consist with which they left Hinton.

A staging area can be very important in making your railroad work in the way that you wish. Some staging yards are set up as stub-end tracks. To me, the disadvantage of this is that trains have to picked up and turned around when they are needed for another run. Another arrangement might be called a through staging area, tying both ends of the railroad together out of sight so that trains can continuously move in and out of staging without being touched.

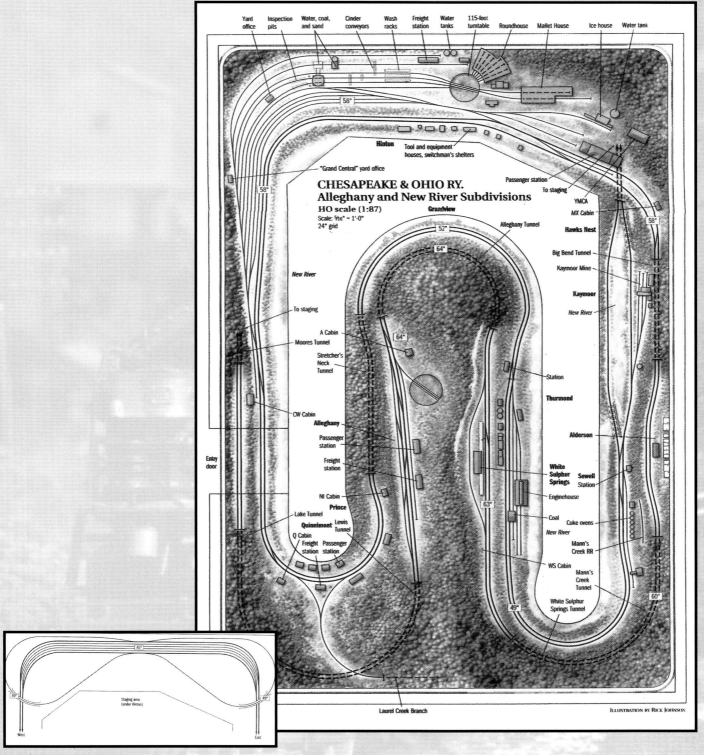

THE LAYOUT AT A GLANCE

Name: Chesapeake & Ohio, Alleghany and New River Subdivisions
Scale: HO (1:87)
Size: 21 x 31 feet
Prototype: C&O Ry.
Locale: Virginia and West Virginia
Era: summer 1938
Layout style: walk-in
Layout height: 45" to 64"
Benchwork: L girder

Roadbed: Homasote over 1/2" plywood
Track: Micro Engineering code 83 flextrack
Turnout minimum: no. 6 Minimum
Radius: 32" Minimum
Grade: 1.75 percent
Length of main line: 350 feet
Scenery Construction: Hydrocal over aluminum screen wire
Control: Zimo Digital Command Control (DCC)
Signals: Integrated Signal System

7. Benchwork

There are numerous types of bench work to support your layout. Without going into detail, the one I have used on three layouts is the L-girder plan. It was first published many years ago by Linn Westcott, the former editor of the Model Railroader magazine. The reason that I have become such a fan of this style is that there always seems to be a ready solution to support anything at any place. This is particularly noteworthy when the railroad is under construction, and you suddenly realize that you need some additional support at some point. I have found with L-girder there is always a base to build on. There are several booklets published by Kalmbach on L-girder.

8. Signals

To me, on a busy Class I railroad, like the C&O, signals make all the difference. In 1938, the C&O manned the interlocking towers (called Cabins on the C&O) 24 hours per day. The operators in these cabins manually controlled the switches at these junctions. In between these points, the mainline was controlled by automatic block signals. We have created both signal situations on our model.

When operating your trains, you must watch and be guided by the signals, just as on the prototype. I rate the signal system as the most interesting part of the railroad.

To duplicate the workings at each cabin, we have created a control panel on the fascia of the layout opposite the model. Here we see the model of CW cabin with its control panel. (Rob Downey)

Quinnimont control cabin atop Quinnimont yard office. The diagram of our control panel shows wye and crossover. (Rob Downey)

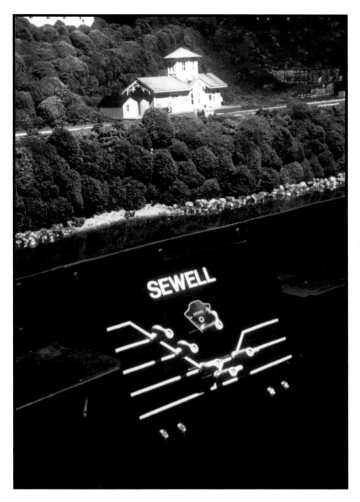

The operator for Thurmond worked at the bay window facing the mainline. The handle to the side of the track diagram controls the train order signal. (Rob Downey)

The cabin controlling turnouts at Sewell is in hexagonal cabin atop the Sewell passenger station. The switch levers indicate the direction in which the switch is thrown. (Rob Downey)

WS is the White Sulphur cabin above the fascia panel. (Rob Downey)

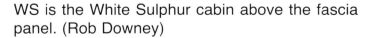

The signals at the junctions are manually controlled by the cabin operator. Between the junctions, the mainline signals are automatic block signals controlled by the train movements just as on the prototype. Here we are showing the four principal signal aspects: Green over red-clear, proceed. (Rule 281) (Rob Downey)

Signal Aspect: Yellow over Red-Approach-Proceed, prepare to stop at next signal, not to exceed medium speed. (Rule 285) (Rob Downey)

Signal Aspect: Red over Yellow-Proceed at restricted speed. (Rule 290) (Rob Downey)

Signal Aspect: Red over Red-Stop. (Rule 292) Train crews must watch and obey the signals. (Rob Downey)

9. Structures

The structures are scratch-built from the original C&O plans, which were obtained from our C&O Historical Society.* There are historical societies for every major and most minor railroads that ever existed in the United States. This presents an endless basis for creating your own prototypical model railroad.

If you have not tried scratch-building structures, I urge you to do so. It was so much fun, I had a hard time stopping when my buildings were all finished. Best of all, your buildings will be uniquely yours, not from a kit.

10. Scenery

Don't overlook scenery. It makes all the difference. You have spent a lot of time on laying track, wiring the railroad, and also perhaps lighting your structures, and a signal system. None of this shows. You've spent the better part of your life under the layout. Now is the time to do something that shows!

For my scenery, I used aluminum screening over wooden supports. Aluminum screens are stiff enough that you can bend it into most of the contours that you wish. I like to cover the screen wire with paper towels dipped in plaster or Hydrocal. This leaves a hollow shell behind the scenery, which is important for tunnels or to reach hidden track.

The "millions" of trees are fast, cheap and easy to make. Start with a little clump of poly fiber (the same material that is stuffed into pillows.) Spray it with cheap black flat paint, then dip it into a container of dark green ground foam, (made by Woodland Scenic). There it is: instant trees.

*Chesapeake & Ohio Historical Society P.O. Box 79, Clifton Forge, VA 24422 Phone: (800) 453-COHS E-mail: cohs@crw.com

Dan Zugelter at the Hinton Depot. (Bernard Kempinski)

Like most kids, my model railroading began with a Lionel train under the Christmas tree. By the late 1930's the Model Builder magazine came out. I was introduced to Frank Ellison and his great Delta Lines railroad. By following his articles, I cut up corrugated cardboard boxes to make my buildings. This became the Middletown Midland Railroad (Middletown was in the middle of the railroad) in the attic of my parents' house.

It all ended in high school and the discovery of girls.

Second childhood began in the 1970's with the Chesapeake and Ohio Historical Society, and what you have just seen.

I hope you have enjoyed this railfanning trip in the summer of 1938.

This is downtown Middletown. The station is in the foreground. There has been an auto accident to the left of the station.

To the left is the Middletown Hotel, next to the Franklin Drug Store. There is a phone booth next to the Barber Shop. A Lionel crossing galeman is in the foreground. These buildings are right out of Model Builder magazine.

As a kid in grade school, I had borrowed my father's Kodak camera, and with no idea what I was doing, took these pictures.

Part of the "suburbs" of Middletown. That's a park on the left.

The main street turned here to cross the double track mainline. Those are the Lionel crossing gates. The watchman's tower was from the magazine article. The red lantern on the cross back in the foreground worked.

Coal mine tipple, with an American Flyer 0-6-0 pushing in coal hoppers. Old faithful, Lionel 2-4-2, coming out of tunnel.

This map is taken a 1938 C&O Public Timetable folder and shows the C&O's main lines as well as the the lines of other railroads that handled though C&O passenger cars. The area under the magnifying glass is the region covered in this book